HINTERLAND

Hinterland offers an answ[er]
question 'what is creative
by showcasing the best ne[w]
the fields of memoir, essay, travel and
food writing, reportage, psychoscape,
biography, flash non-fiction and more.

Our pages bring together work by
established, award-winning authors
alongside new writers, many of whom
we are thrilled to publish for the first time
and whose work, we promise, will merit
your full attention.

Often, the pieces you'll find in Hinterland
will straddle the boundaries between
strands and be difficult to classify:
we see this as a strength. Hinterland
intends to challenge, move, entertain
and, above all, be a fantastic read.

WELCOME TO ISSUE 6

Advocates for Hinterland:
Nathan Hamilton, Kathryn Hughes,
Helen Smith, Rebecca Stott, Ian Thomson

Editorial Team
Editors-In-Chief – Freya Dean & Andrew Kenrick
Art Direction & Design – Tom Hutchings
Business Support – Ben Watkins
Contributing Editors – Susan Karen Burton, Yin F. Lim
Proofreaders – Susan K. Burton, Aaron Deary, Margaret Hedderman,
              Yin F. Lim and Stephen Massil

Submissions
Hinterland is committed to paying writers and artists for all work we publish.
Please send us your work via Submittable:
hinterlandnonfiction.submittable.com
We accept submissions year-round and endeavour to reply within 4 months.
We regret we are unable to provide feedback.
There is a small fee of £3 per submission.

Subscriptions
An annual subscription to Hinterland (four issues, print and digital)
costs £40 U.K., £44 Europe, £54 Rest-of-world.
Digital subscription only, £20.
Please visit our website for full details.

Distribution
Hinterland is distributed worldwide by NBN International.
For all trade orders contact +44 (0) 1752 202301
orders@nbninternational.com

Advertising
Please see our website for current rates, or to discuss sponsorship please
contact us at hinterlandnonfiction@gmail.com

Acknowledgments
The Editors gratefully acknowledge financial contributions from
the UEA Publishing Project.

Find Hinterland online at
www.hinterlandnonfiction.com
or contact us: hinterlandnonfiction@gmail.com

ISBN: 978-1-911343-83-7
ISSN (Print): 2632-136X
ISSN (Online): 2632-1378

HINTERLAND

THE BEST NEW CREATIVE NON-FICTION

Issue 6
2020

Issue 6

Editorial

Here at Hinterland, the label that we apply to our favoured genre – 'non-fiction' – is often a dissatisfying one, defined more by what it is not rather than what it is. That we often append to it the word 'creative' adds another unwelcome distinction, with the implication that there is a whole world of uncreative non-fiction out there too. This binary mode extends to authors: are you a novelist or do you write non-fiction? The suggestion being that you either make stuff up or you are a stickler for the facts, and that the two are mutually exclusive. This issue we are tackling these contradictions head-on, under the teasing label of a 'non-fiction fiction special'.

And so Heather Martin writes about her very real biography of novelist Lee Child, the creator of the very fictional Jack Reacher. When author Nick Bradley chose Tokyo as the setting of his debut

Freya Dean is of Dutch-British descent. She graduated from UEA's Creative Writing MA where she received the Lorna Sage award and, the same year, was an Elizabeth Kostova Foundation Finalist. Recent work features in *The Real Story*, *Visual Verse* and UEA's Anthology series.

novel *The Cat and The City*, he mined the experience of nearly a decade's worth of daily commutes in the city, documented in his photo essay here. Much like the subject of Ashley Hickson-Lovence's second novel, the focus of his piece for Hinterland is a real character, the Norwich City striker Ruel Fox. Elsewhere, in our regular archive feature, Yin F. Lim unearths correspondence between Malaysian-born novelist Tash Aw and his editor, shedding light on the writing process, and Susan Karen Burton interviews Helen Smith about her biography of literary editor Edward Garnett.

That's not all, of course – you'll also find a fantastic selection of non-fiction from all our talented writers, tackling an all-too real array of stories including terrorism, drug-fuelled blackouts, toys abandoned by the roadside and the songs of Neil Young.

We hope you enjoy!

Freya & Andrew

Andrew Kenrick has worked as an archaeologist and an archivist, a writer and an editor. He is currently studying for a PhD at the University of East Anglia, where he also teaches English Literature and Publishing.

Contributors

Peter Bethanis (*The Humma*) has published poems, essays, and art in several journals including *Poetry*, *Country Journal*, *Tar River Poetry* and *Atticus*, among others. He has won the Eve of St. Agnes Poetry Prize, and is the author of two books, *Dada and Surrealism for Beginners* and *American Future*.

Nick Bradley (*Overexposed*) is a graduate of both the MA and the PhD in Creative and Critical Writing programs at UEA. His debut novel *The Cat and The City* was published by Atlantic Books in the UK in June 2020, North America in September, and is currently being translated into multiple languages. It was chosen for the BBC Radio 2 Book Club with Jo Whiley, and has received praise in *The Times* and *The Guardian* amongst others. For a decade, Nick lived and worked in Japan.

Susan Karen Burton (*In Conversation with…*) holds two doctorates, in history from the University of Sussex and in creative and critical writing from the University of East Anglia. She writes primarily about Japan, where she lived and worked for 14 years, latterly as an associate professor at several Japanese universities. Her work has appeared in *Times Higher Education, The Telegraph, The Manchester Review, Words and Women,* and *Going Down Swinging.* She is also the co-author of two books in Japanese. She is the winner of the 2020 New Welsh Writing Award's Rheidol Prize for prose with a Welsh theme or setting, and is currently writing a book about the Welsh in Japan.

Meg Freer (*Tbilisi Sounds in Transit*) grew up in Montana and has worked in book publishing. She now teaches piano, takes photos and enjoys the outdoors year-round in Ontario. Her photos, poems and prose have been published in journals such as *Ruminate, Vallum Contemporary Poetry, Young Ravens Literary Review, Eastern Iowa Review,* and *Rat's Ass Review.* In 2017 she attended the Summer Literary Seminars in Tbilisi, Republic of Georgia. Her poetry has won awards and have been shortlisted for several contests in both the U.S. and Canada.

Tom Hutchings (*Chilled Breeze*) is our in-house designer and photographer, despite being based in London. He's recently moved to work freelance full-time so if you have any graphics that need designing, why not drop him a line through: thorngraphicdesign.com

Alice Jolly's (*Big Hugs and Kisses*) most recent novel *Mary Ann Sate, Imbecile* (Unbound) was runner up for the Rathbones Folio Prize and was longlisted for the Ondaatje Prize. Alice has also won the Pen Ackerley Prize for memoir and the V.S. Pritchett Memorial Prize for a short story. Her stories have appeared in *Prospect*, *Ploughshares*, *The Manchester Review*, *Litro* and *Fairlight*. She teaches creative writing at Oxford University.

Ashley Hickson-Lovence (*Nearly City*) is a writer and educator from Hackney, currently based in Norwich. While working as a secondary school English teacher, he completed his MA in Creative Writing and Publishing and is currently completing his PhD in Creative and Critical Writing at the University of East Anglia. His debut novel *The 392* was released with OWN IT! in April 2019. His second novel *Your Show*, a novelisation of the early life and career of former Premier League football referee Uriah Rennie, is to be released with Faber in Spring 2022.

Yin F Lim (*From the Archive*) is a Malaysian-born writer and editor living in Norwich. Her creative non-fiction work on family, food and migration has appeared in *Hinterland, Porridge, American Writers Review's* 'Art in the Time of Covid-19' special issue and in the anthology *Who Are We Now? A Collection of True Stories about Brexit.* She holds a Creative Non-Fiction MA from the University of East Anglia.

Heather Martin (*Lee Child: A Geek and a Nerd in Many Ways*) was born in West Australia and moved to London aged sixteen with the idea of becoming a musician. Four years of guitar-playing and a Venezuelan folk group later, she wound up reading languages at Cambridge instead. This led to lectureships in twentieth-century Spanish and Latin American literature first at Hull, then at King's College London, and thence to a career in teaching, writing and translating. While researching *The Reacher Guy*, her biography of Lee Child, she was based for a year at the Department of Comparative Literature at the Graduate Center, City University New York.

Matthew Mead (*An Escarpment*) is a craftsperson and writer. His work has appeared in *Textual Practice, Photography & Culture, Cabinet* and elsewhere. He lives in London and can be found @other_objects.

Nathan Munday (*Bear Stalking in the Bucegi*) is a Welsh writer from Carmarthenshire. In 2016 he won the M. Wynn Thomas New Scholars Prize and came second in the New Welsh Writing Awards with his creative non-fiction book *Seven Days: A Pyrenean Adventure*, published by Parthian in 2017. He has also been placed twice for poetry in the Terry Hetherington Awards (2019, 2020). When he's not writing and reading, he enjoys mountains; and works for Christian Aid.

Tom Price (*Home*) is a pseudonym.

Helen Smith (*In Conversation with…*) is the author of *An Uncommon Reader: A Life of Edward Garnett* which was Sunday Times Literature Book of the Year, winner of the Biographers' Club Prize and a RSl/Jerwood award for Non-Fiction. The book was shortlisted for the Simply Foxed First Biography Prize. She has published articles in various publications ranging from *The Wall Street Journal* to *Literature in Translation*. She lives in Norfolk and teaches non-fiction at the University of East Anglia.

Sahanika Ratnayake
(*Three People Lost Their Lives*) is a PhD student in Philosophy at the University of Cambridge. She was born in Sri Lanka and grew up in New Zealand and Australia, and has lived in the UK for the past two years. Her work has appeared in *Aeon*, *3AM Magazine* and *VICE*, as well as Australasian literary journals such as *Overland* and *Poetry New Zealand*.

Alexander Williamson
(*On the Beach*) is a writer and photographer. He has an MA in Modern and Contemporary Literature from Birkbeck, University of London, and a PhD in English from Birkbeck. His first book is, *Laughing Stock*, an autofictional memoir. His poems have appeared, sporadically, in *Aesthetica*, *Aspidistra*, *Dream Catcher*, *Magma*, *Orbis* and *South Bank Poetry*. He is currently working on a novel about Henry Miller titled *The Cancerian*.

HINTERLAND

At Hinterland we are committed to publishing the best in creative non-fiction from around the globe.

We are always thrilled to feature work from established, well-known authors but have a particular interest in discovering new voices and in pieces that sit outside the usual categories: we ask only that it be a work of non-fiction.

We operate an open, year-round submissions policy and aim to read all work submitted within three months.

We pay for all the work that we publish and receive frequent interest from agents and publishers regarding our contributors.

Please send us your best work and we will endeavour to find a place for it.

Guidelines for submissions

- Submissions should be made via Submittable only. Please follow the link below:

- A small fee of £3 per submission applies to non-subscribers. Subscribers enjoy the benefit of submitting their work for free.

- All work should be new, previously unpublished material. If your work is subsequently accepted elsewhere, please kindly let us know.

- Pieces should not run to more than 5000 words. We accept anything from 500 words (very short pieces will be considered for our flash non-fiction slot). We also accept extracts from longer works, or works in progress.

- We warmly embrace writing on any topic, or from any genre, we ask only that it falls somewhere in the realm of non-fiction writing.

- Your work will be considered for all upcoming issues; it might help you to know that we operate a 3-4 month editorial lead time.

- We regret that, due to the number of submissions received, we cannot provide feedback.

hinterland.submittable.com/submit

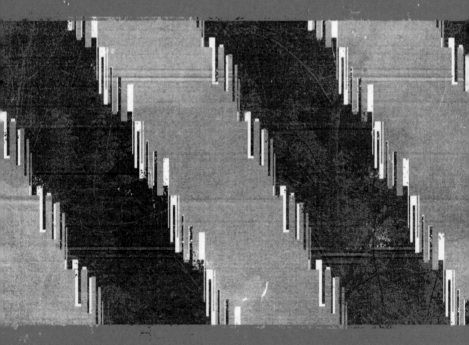

PENGUIN BOOKS

COMING UP FOR AIR
—
GEORGE ORWELL

YOU ARE HERE

THE RINGS OF SATURN   W.G. SEBALD

A FIELD GUIDE TO GETTING LOST
REBECCA SOLNIT

HINTERLAND

The Humma

Peter Bethanis

As a boy, I was sentenced to a forty-minute bus route that weaved up and down the hills of rural Maine. Our bus driver was Old Man Bennett. He had a green work outfit that bore the nickname 'Buzz' on a red and white patch sewn on his chest pocket. The back of his head was bald and shaped like a light bulb, and his eyes occasionally glanced up into the horizontal mirror above his head, trying to spot kids shooting spit balls.

I was District #92's spitball king. Each ride, Bennett's eyes darted back and forth from that mirror, trying to spot smugglers as the loud, rowdy faces and thumping feet pushed and shoved their way down the narrow aisle. Old Man Bennett never once caught the straw I secretly stashed in my sock.

Getting to the back seat of the bus was like winning the lottery. Kids flipped and flopped like salmon trying to swim upstream in an effort to dive into its secluded cavern. From the back seat, we traded baseball cards and globbed wads of pink gum in our mouths. Gum that had lost its flavor was stuck like putty under the seats.

After clumping the wad of tasteless paper in my mouth, I loved kneading the wet ammo between my fingers into deadly pellets the size of orange pits. My trick was to load three or four pellets at once and send a spray of seeds at the enemy, always careful not to suck in and swallow one.

All the spitball fighters looked forward to the long driveway of Andrea White. She was a tall girl with long brown hair that she constantly brushed from her eyes. Most of the kids called her The Humma. A humma was known to mean the ugliest cow, or a calf born with three legs, or one eye.

Whenever Andrea's lanky figure slinked shyly down the aisle, a chant of 'Humma, Humma, Humma,' started up until Old Man Bennett's evil glance shot up into the mirror and he shouted, 'Settle down!'

When the Humma got on the bus, it was like having an antelope in our sights. I was the only one to ever hit her right between the eyes. Besides spit balls, Billy Jenkins dared to sneak up and thwack the back of her ear lobes, turning them bright red.

One day when school was cancelled early because of a snowstorm, the bus was crazier than ever. Having won the back seat in a reckless dive, I sat globbing paper in my mouth, determined to win the spitball war. Jimmy Urbink had hit me in the forehead, and it felt like a bee sting. Billy Jenkins claimed that he had hit the Humma between the eyes, but I didn't see it. Then he sent a clean shot that pricked the back of her neck, sending a chain of laughter down both rows of the bus. Old Man Bennett was preoccupied with the slippery roads as we despatched hundreds of wads of paper at one another.

As the bus pulled into the turn-around point, the wheels began to spin. Getting out of school early, having the back seat, and now being stuck swirled in my head. After several more attempts to pull out, Bennett took a shovel from behind his seat, and as his foot stepped out the door, a barrage of crayons, pencils, superballs, and even a sneaker went flying off like rockets and fireworks.

I spotted an apple on the floor beneath the seat across from me. When I picked it up, it was bruised and soft, and I ground it into the grimy floor. My arm coiled back and hurled it through the air into the storm of objects. Then everything came to a halt as the apple struck with a dull thud against the head of the Humma.

For a brief second, silence loomed over the bus. I stood silent and felt my empty fingertips still tingling as the rest of the bus chanted 'Humma, Humma, Humma!' Then her face turned, and her neck tried to lower and return to the book she had been reading.

Just then the old man returned with the snow shovel in his hand, looked at the girl with some of the dirt from the apple still smeared on her forehead, and muttered something under his breath.

The whole bus grew silent – his expression never looked more stern. He ordered everyone to stand up. A part of me stood as still as I could while another part felt as though I'd swallowed a pillow full of feathers. Old Man Bennett worked his way to the back of the bus, the shovel still in his hand.

I wish I could finish by saying that Old Man Bennett wrapped the shovel around my neck. Or maybe how I could have asked Andrea if she was hurt, or said something to her, anything. But that's not what happened.

I do remember watching her getting off the bus, her brown hair disappearing into the woods and snow as she walked up her long driveway. Just as I remember getting off the bus that day, sticking my bare hand in the snow to stop the tingling; and then standing alone with my thoughts and making a snowball, tossing it half-heartedly at our mailbox, and missing. ▪

An Escarpment

Matthew Mead

Back then, I did not know the names of the trees;
but I knew the holly that scratched at our palms and
ankles, and where to find the thickest canopy when
the rain set in. Sometimes, when the rain fell hard,
and it was too early to trudge home, I would slip
into a hollow under the wide trunk of a tree that
came down in the great storm of '87. As a child, you
imagine that a storm is a thing of one night, but the
trunk still lies there now.

Where the banks of the woods were steepest, we
climbed on all fours, using momentum to propel us
upwards. Here, the borders between the woods and
the back gardens belonging to wealthier families were
unclear. It seems remarkable now that there were
no fences. Perhaps they too enjoyed the uncertainty.
Here, I would sometimes explore an outbuilding,
and take a long-abandoned crate, sheet of tarpaulin,
or roll of barbed wire to enhance a camp.

But on the day I'm thinking of now, I climbed to
an escarpment that I'd never found before. It was
the best time of year and the dry earth kicked up
in clouds as I dug the toes of my plimsoles into the
soft powder. And then, opening up maybe as much
as fifteen metres below me, I saw a large house with
a garden in full bloom. It was well groomed, with a
tidy lawn, but became wild at the edges. The house
– large and suburban – was impossibly comfortable

compared to our own two-up, two-down. Although the doors and windows were open, there wasn't a soul around. I lay on my belly, in the cool of the shade, with my chin in my hands, and watched nothing for unmeasured time, as transfixed as if I were peering into the complete and intimate world of a stereograph.

One summer, children a few years older than us achieved the mysterious feat of rigging a rope swing over a high branch. For a short time, the rope swing was all I could think of – the exhilaration of rising up into the air as the bank fell away below, and the exhilaration also of being with children a few years my senior. Returning alone one day, I stood looking up at singed fibres of blue nylon rope, a metre or more above my reach. We were learning to read the signs, to discern echoes of trouble from real threat: the woods were where my brother found a dead cat in a plastic sack; where the friend of a neighbour, who later died of an overdose, chased me swinging a snooker ball in a sock; where a homeless man, drunk and infuriated to find me and a friend camping on a mattress that was his home, set fire to his only possessions to smoke us out.

No matter how much I explored, I never again came to the view of the house, and the garden in bloom. Over the years I reconciled myself to the unreality of the experience. The woods were not that big. As an adult, the whole area could be explored in less than an hour, and its boundaries clearly defined. There was no such view, no such house. Turning this memory over in my mind was like reading a short story by Hermann Hesse, or looking at the perfectly childish lines of a Klee painting. It was a dream that promised to reveal the forgotten secrets of childhood.

And then, a year or two ago, my brother said to me, *do you remember the time we climbed to the top of the woods? To a ridge we had never before found? And we looked down on a beautiful house, with a wild garden, and lay on our bellies, in the shade, watching nothing happen?* And neither of us knows whose dream this is. ∎

Tbilisi Sounds in Transit

Meg Freer

A typical summer day begins with vibrations of a single, bright turquoise wall on a building; a yellow bird singing in a courtyard cage; the muffled bubbling of water from the hookah a man smokes in the nearby café; neighborhood sounds of classical violin practice and jazz piano.

All big cities are noisy, and parts of Tbilisi, capital of the Republic of Georgia, are particularly so. Impatient drivers jostle for position on the twisty, one-way streets where every swerve of a car is punctuated by short beeps of the horn. But old Tbilisi is alive with other sounds besides traffic. Move away from the busy and constant construction and reconstruction of ancient buildings, and there are church bells, the deafening buzz of cicadas, and men shouting while they toss the largest watermelons I've ever seen from the back of a van into a stack to sell by the side of the road.

The city fully wakes late at night when temperatures cool off. Garbage trucks collect trash at midnight from big communal bins, construction work picks up, cafés and restaurants are packed. A piano sculpture in a park by the river has keys that make no sound, but dancing fountains light up and spout in patterns and rhythms timed perfectly to match recorded music. Whole families, including toddlers and babies, are out walking, filling alleyways and parks with music and talk. I wonder when the children ever sleep, until I notice how quiet the afternoons are. **H**

Bear stalking in the Bucegi

Nathan Munday

We spent the first night in Sinaia, and ate in a place that promised 'grilled meats'; most of it was pork sausage, I think. As we ate, we noticed a stretched-out bearskin behind us. Its splat-like embrace of the whitewashed wall disturbed me.

After dinner, we spread the map across the table. Romania is torqued by the Carpathian Mountains, the Bucegi a link in that grand necklace.

My father was the peak bagger, eccentric and very English. My friend was our translator, eccentric and very Welsh. And I was the bear stalker – a combination of Welsh/English eccentricity.

The first hill we ascended was Mount Omu (2505m). The ski-scarred slopes soon gave way to a strange dwarf pine forest. If there were teddies in these woods, they'd be small and unknown. The distant mountains shimmered like islands in a shallow sea. The climb was easy enough and the snow still lurked on the hillside; its white robes transformed the bareness into an elegant vista. Our own shadows clashed with the clouds. Their darkness reminded me of the Strigoi – old Romanian devils. They've long gone, as has Ceausescu. But the bears are still here.

There were no trees up high. I wanted to go down into the Transylvanian woods and look for bears, but night drove us, like a powerful sheepdog, into the refuge.

Twenty Israelis, a South African, some Romanians, and three Brits; we huddled in an L-shaped bed. The old Turkish boiler gave us a sticky night. The Israelis were condemned for cooking their food in the dorm, while the South African tapped a lightbulb with his nail, unwilling to accept the lack of electricity. The night was made worse when one of the Romanians broke wind again and again.

We descended towards Bran, visited Dracula's Castle, and even had a night in Brasov. But the only bears were the ones on the postcard racks, growling in the wind, as they rotated like those Tibetan prayer wheels.

After a day of sightseeing, the stalking continued. I'd never experienced woods like Transylvania before. The greens platted over one another like leaves of a grand book; tall beech trees, not swaying, but slowly ascending with the hill and lining the high cols.

Then Dad found some fresh dung next to a large paw-print. We stood around the print like Indiana Jones, Sallah, and Marcus Brody. Tree to tree, sweating, twigs snapping – it was great. At one point, the rattling of a bush startled me… but it was only a deer.

We spent the last evening eating venison in a Roma forest restaurant; swooned by a tarantella played on three accordions. We headed back to Bucharest on an old Communist train. ▉

17 May 2004

Dear Cindy,

Thanks so much for your comments. I've spent the last month working on your suggestions, and have made numerous changes to take these into account. In particular, I think the second part of the novel has benefited from these relatively small but very important tweaks. I also looked at how to make the eventual relationship between Kunichika and Johnny that bit clearer, because I agree that it's important the reader is left with no doubt as to Johnny's ultimate duplicity (as well as the reasons for it). Now that Nicholas has finished editing too, I feel that I've done all that I want to do with this book – or rather, all that I can do with it.

I've agonised over the ending. I read your comments over and over again, and tested out several different ways to bring greater resolution to the end, but none of them seemed to work. First of all, I experimented with your suggestion, which was to bring Jasper back at the end of the novel for a short fourth narrative later on in his life. Now that he had read the diary, his understanding of his father was much changed. The Johnny he knew was not the real Johnny. But this – like all the other variations I attempted – didn't feel right. As I worked through your editorial comments, it became clear to me that my original vision for this novel would not work if we saw Jasper reading Snow's diary and finding out about Johnny's involvement with Kunichika and Peter. The ramifications of this would be too great to handle within the scope of this novel; Jasper's emotional response to this cannot be contained in a single section at the end. It would also change completely the tone of his Part I narrative, taking the tragedy out of it. As I have left it, we know that Jasper will read the diary and see the photograph that Peter gives him at the funeral; but we do not see him do those things. The moment we witness these acts, the poignancy is lost.

The entire structure of the novel is based on silences. Our understanding of the truth rests heavily on the fact that we know things that the characters do not know of each other. Silence affects the voice of the narratives, so that we know there is something missing. Johnny never has a narrative voice; he remains silent to the end of the novel. I have tried very hard to give this book a revised conclusion, one that does not disrupt the balance created by this silence, but such an ending has eluded me. I can't see a way to do it without altering the very fabric of the novel.

I do understand that this might, as you point out, result in an unsatisfactory read, a lack of 'pay-off.' I have thought about this a lot, and it is a risk I am willing to take because I feel very strongly that any lack of resolution that the reader feels will be compensated for by the sense of loss and mystery that inhabit the novel. I want the reader to be haunted, to be somewhat disconcerted, as the characters are. The answers are all there, and, with your help, I've tightened things up a little to make sure that the reader is never lost.

As far as Snow is concerned, I have made a number of changes as you suggested, in order to cut down on what seems like vagueness. I agree that we must be aware of exactly what her predicament is, and what her choices entail. I have, however,

Letter from Tash Aw to his editor Cindy Spiegel

by Yin F Lim

Editors play an important role in helping shape a manuscript into the book that finally ends up in the readers' hands. Gordon Lish and his judicious pruning of Raymond Carver's short stories have been credited for the unflinching, pared-back style for which Carver is now celebrated. According to literary history, Thomas Wolfe's voluminous manuscripts – the typescript of his first novel apparently ran to over 300,000 words – would never have seen the light of day if not for the patience and persistence of his editor Max Perkins[1].

But the relationship between author and editor can be fraught with much tension. This often arises from the sense of gratitude that the author feels for their editor's input, battling with their apprehensions about how much the final edit will resemble their own, original work. Navigating this relationship is enough of a challenge for established writers, let alone for a first-time novelist faced with revisions that could alter the very essence of their manuscript.

This dilemma is captured in a May 2004 letter that Malaysian author Tash Aw wrote to his editor Cindy Spiegel at Riverhead Books, the US publisher of his debut novel *The Harmony Silk Factory*. In it, Aw

---

1 Morrison, B (2005). 'Black day for the blue pencil'. The Guardian.
   https://www.theguardian.com/books/2005/aug/06/featuresreviews.guardianreview1

stopped short of giving her a more emotionally forthright and articulate voice throughout. One of the things I wanted to do with her section was to play with the expectations we normally have when reading a diary in a novel, especially one written by a woman, ie the expectations of intimacy, even sentimentalism. I wanted to give Snow many of the things men normally have, so that her journal is, firstly, a straightforward record of a road-trip adventure, the kind of things usually enjoyed by men. Secondly, I wanted her not to spill her emotions onto the page, but rather imply them, have them lurking slightly beneath the surface so that – as we do with men – we sometimes have to guess rather than be told. There is also the issue of authenticity of voice. It is highly unlikely that a Malaysian-Chinese woman in 1941 would be particularly forthright or articulate about her feelings, even to herself. Snow's relative boldness is already a problem for her parents. So I think it's right that she remains a little bit reticent (there's that silence again). I have made quite a few adjustments, though, and I hope her agony is properly conveyed.

I've also made a few subtle changes to try and clarify the paternity question, mindful of the fact that I can't change the ending substantially. The scenes at the end of Parts II and III involving Snow and the (attempted) rape have made been less confusing, so that it is slightly clearer what happens. I hope this compensates somewhat for the absence of a comprehensive answer at the end of the novel.

I have very much appreciated your comments. They have made me see my novel in ways I didn't see before, and forced me to think about the things I'm trying to do. I have considered and reconsidered, and taken into account all of what you've said. Where I have resisted your suggestions, I have done so only after thorough brain-wracking.

One more thing to add. If, after you've read the above, you still feel very strongly that you'd like *something* at the end of the novel, I have written a one-page epilogue, narrated by Jasper, which doesn't give anything away, but tells us that he has read the diary and seen the photograph. It indicates that much time has passed and that he is more confused that ever; answers in life are never straightforward. I don't think this is a solution to the novel, and I would prefer the end to stay as it is, but if you feel that you'd like to see this epilogue in the American edition, I'd certainly show it to you. I shan't, however, be offering it to Nick or to any of the other editors.

The editing process hasn't been a breeze, but I do feel that the book has benefited enormously from it. I have benefited too. I feel I know my novel better than I ever have, and I am more convinced of it than before. Thank you for being so involved in it.

Please do ring – it would be good to chat.

Best regards

Tash

expresses his appreciation to Spiegel, noting how much her editorial input has benefitted his book. But he also reveals how he had 'agonised' over her suggestions for modifying the ending of his novel, to achieve what Spiegel considered a better 'pay-off' for the reader. Aw eventually decided to resist her suggestions and kept his ending as it was originally written.

> **'The editing process hasn't been a breeze, but I do feel the book has benefited enormously from it. I have benefited too. I feel I know my novel better than I ever have.' – Tash Aw**

What is notable from Aw's letter is the strength of his belief in his work and the experience he wanted to create for the reader of *The Harmony Silk Factory*, a historical novel set in 1940s Malaya. The confidence of this then-debut author is evident in how he offers Spiegel the option of an epilogue to address some of her concerns, while making it clear that this would be for the American edition only.

Published in 2005, *The Harmony Silk Factory* went on to win both the Whitbread First Novel Award and the Commonwealth Writers' Prize for Best First Novel in the South East Asia and South Pacific region. It was also long-listed for the 2005 Man Booker Prize. Such accolades are testament to the fact that, while editors can certainly help improve a manuscript, equally crucial is the author's conviction to stand by the vision they have for their work. **H**

32 Hinterland

LEE CHILD

A GEEK AND A NERD, IN A LOT OF WAYS

by Heather Martin

In July 2017 Lee Child wrote a short story for an anthology in support of the American Civil Liberties Union. I was in New York at the time. He gave me a printout. There is something very precious about being the first reader of a story hot off the press.

The story was called 'New Blank Document'. It was about a black piano player from some 'no-account shithole in the Florida panhandle' who chose voluntary exile in Paris after serving in the Second World War. Cuthbert Jackson was a man of mystery, and of very few words, which only increased his fame. The little he said he considered plain common sense, but when translated into French he sounded like Socrates. Some guy wrote a book about his 'five-word answer to a question about the likely future of mankind'. His record sales went through the roof. A French magazine wanted to write a full-scale biography, serialised over thirteen weeks. The narrator of 'New Blank Document' was a hack journalist, writing stories to pay the rent and, if he was lucky, put food on the table, recruited by the magazine for background information on Jackson's family.

It wasn't this story that gave me the idea. Maybe the other way round. Lee already knew I wanted to write his biography. He knew I'd visited Coventry, where he was born, and Birmingham, where he grew up. He was sceptical. He wasn't worried about literary legacy. His job was done; he'd provided for his family, and generations of descendants if need be, which was what society had programmed him to do. He didn't need, or even want, to be remembered. 'No one will buy it,' he said. 'No one will want to read about me.' If I did write it, he added, could I please keep an eye on the bigger sociological picture, so it wasn't just about him.

But we were talking, and it was a long conversation, already stretching back more than a year. And when Lee spoke, and I listened, it was like he was telling me a story and my job was to write it all down. I wanted to remember, even if he didn't. I was writing *The Reacher Guy* before either of us knew it.

Our conversation had begun in an unexpected way. Lee knew I was a Hispanist. One day he sent me a copy of one of his novels in Spanish translation, and on the title page he'd written: 'Let me know if it's any good.' So I did. I told him how his syntax had been smoothed over and normalised in ways not required by grammar, how verbless fragments had been 'corrected', how short sentences had been joined and long ones broken up. I told him how it betrayed Reacher's laconic style, and how it didn't read like Lee Child, which was a shame, because what defines Lee Child is his voice;

and doubly a shame, because Spanish is a flexible and accommodating language, already in many ways adapted to the forms and rhythms of English. For a while I nurtured the desire to translate his next novel into Spanish myself, even making a start on the first few chapters, but I soon realised that the idioms would defeat me, if not the syntax. Instead, when Argentina's indie press Blatt & Ríos stepped up to the plate, I contented myself with translating the reviews into English. Eventually, Lee gave me his copy of the elegantly produced *Noche Caliente*, a translation by Aldo Giacometti of his 2012 and 2013 novellas, *Deep Down* and *High Heat*, and once again, asked what I thought of it. He wanted to know whether to press the button on a long-term deal. I liked Giacometti. He got it. When I read his Spanish, I could still hear Lee's voice. *Lee Child en español. ¡Perfecto!*

This was a still-living author, and I knew him. Many of the words in *The Reacher Guy* are his, whether spoken or written

Conversation is the core of this biography. It's only natural that it should be, in the same way it was natural to refer to my subject by his first name (anyway, I wanted 'child' to preserve its other meanings). This was a still-living author, and I knew him. Many of the words in *The Reacher Guy* are his, whether spoken or written. Lee was adamant that he would never write an autobiography or memoir. Partly this was for existential reasons: life was meaningless, biography would invest it with some kind of meaning, and he simply didn't see himself as that important – no single human being was. Partly because he feared boredom: he preferred invention to revision. And partly because – as he often explained – certain things were easier to say from a third-person perspective. He liked the fact that I was Australian. I was an outsider, less likely to be steeped in the prejudices and preconceptions of the British class system that he believed had straitjacketed his parents and predestined him for mediocrity, which in turn had provoked him to revolt, and either way had defined the course of his life.

But that didn't mean the idea of autobiographical writing was alien to him. Increasingly, as he grew in literary stature, he was asked to reflect on his own life. As always, he was the master of register.

Entertaining an audience: 'After ten years as Aston Villa's top scorer and a brief marriage to Charlize Theron ...'

Renewing contact with an old friend: 'Not much to report . . . 18 years at Granada TV, which was a fun job, but it all fell apart in the upheavals of the 1990s, and I became a writer as a desperation move, but fortunately it worked out OK.'

Recounting the banal minutiae of a transatlantic voyage (2013 introduction to *Running Blind* for The Mysterious Press):

We went by ocean liner for two reasons: we had a dog, and we didn't want to put her in an airplane hold, and because insurance on container consignments was compulsory, expensive, and pro-rata with the value of the contents. The ocean liner allowed unlimited baggage [. . .] so we bought trunks and hand-carried the most expensive stuff, thereby lowering the container insurance to the point where the saving more or less paid for the liner tickets.

Writing a letter to his late Irish grandfather (1418now.org.uk) on the centenary of the declaration of the First World War:

> You don't know me yet, but I have things to tell you. You're about to go back, and I'm sorry to say it's going to be worse than ever this time. You're going to be wounded, I'm afraid. Very badly. But you'll survive. You'll make it home. You have to, you see. Forty years from now you'll become my grandfather.
>
> Not that home will be a bed of roses. Wages will be down, and three men will fight for every job. At times you'll be cold, and at times you'll be hungry. And if you say anything, they'll come at you with truncheons.
>
> And then it will get worse. There are some lean years coming. And I'm sorry, but along the way you'll realise: the war didn't end. It

was just a lull. You'll have to do it all again.
This time your son will have to go, not you.
You don't know him yet, but you will. But
don't worry. He'll get back too. He has to.
You're my grandfather, remember?

And I'll be born in a different world.
There will be jobs for everyone. They'll
be building houses. You'll go to the doctor
whenever you want. I'll go to school. I'll get
free orange juice. You'll get free walking
sticks. But most of all we'll get peace.
Finally, year after year. I will never go to
war, you know. I will never have to. The
first time I go to France will be a trip with
my school.

So go back now, and play your tiny part
in the great drama, and sustain yourself
by knowing: it comes out well in the end.
I promise.

Or addressing the readers of the *New York Times*
('No. 1 in America', 2016):

We had no bombs falling on our houses,
and no knocks on our doors in the middle
of the night. [. . .] We were very lucky.

But it was very boring. Britain was gray,
exhausted, physically ruined and financially
crippled. The factories were humming, but

everything went for export. We needed
foreign currency to pay down monstrous war
debt. Domestic life was pinched and austere.

Not that we knew. We didn't miss what
we'd never had. Worse for us was a kind of
mental and emotional deadness that we felt
all around. There was nothing left for us.
There was nothing in the future. It was all
in the past. History was over. Britain's finest
hour had been 1940, and now the clock was
slowly winding down.

In this article, Lee pictures his parents in June 1940.
Though one is in Belfast and the other in Otley he
brings them together in a single potent image that
has the rich, fixed patina of a historic oil painting. It
is as though their fate is predetermined, their young
lives over before they have even met.

My father was then 16, listening to
Churchill on the radio, heading inexorably
for the army, sitting across the room from
my one-legged grandfather, from the first
war. My mother was 14, a schoolgirl near
an industrial city, told to listen for planes
and get under the table.

They survived, with millions of others,
young and free, but the sustained six-year
emotional thunderclap they had endured left
them weary and exhausted. The war and its

winning (with a little help here and there, they would sometimes grudgingly admit) were both a horror and an achievement unlikely ever to be paralleled, ever again, and therefore anything that came by afterward was necessarily an anti-climax.

I found the range and rhetoric of his discourse compelling in all its forms. The unique mix of humour, self-deprecation and pathos, the sweeping historical vision, the painterly and poetic touches, the idiosyncratic turn of phrase, lingeringly old-fashioned without ever being quaint. Who else, I wondered, would write 'the war and its winning'? The words could not be simpler, but who else would think of combining them in precisely that way? Lee Child had many imitators, but there was a touch of divine madness to his writing that could never be reproduced, that he speculatively attributed to the liberating influence of cannabis.

Lee Child had many imitators, but there was a touch of divine madness to his writing that could never be reproduced

I made as much room as possible for Lee's words and his madness – though I had to stop myself referring back to his introductions to The Mysterious Press editions of his novels because I felt paralysed by the efficiency of his narrative. But he wasn't the only person I was talking to. I spoke to school friends from Cherry Orchard Primary and King Edward's. I spoke to his Sixth Form English teacher, who also ran the dramatic society for which the teenage Jim acted as sound and lighting technician. I spoke to fellow students from Sheffield University, colleagues from Granada Television, and neighbours from Kirkby Lonsdale, to his agent Darley Anderson and his first editor David Highfill, then to his Hollywood film agent, Steve Fisher. Most of these people were not bestselling authors, yet I found myself entranced by their individual modes of expression. I had no desire to smooth over their syntax with bland paraphrase. Perhaps this was the frustrated novelist in me, but I suspect it had more to do with my past life as a teacher. In the classroom every child counts, and no detail is too small to matter. Lee might have the lead role, but the supporting cast mattered too, and they must have their say. Mine would be a polyphonic text, with different characters complementing and sometimes contradicting each other like the instruments in an orchestra. It was a way of triangulating my perception of Lee, a means of testing his recollection of events against alternative viewpoints, and perhaps approximating the truth somewhere between.

I knew it could only ever be an approximation. 'Lee Child', the artist formerly known as Jim Grant, was living proof of the biographical illusion

I knew it could only ever be an approximation. 'Lee Child', the artist formerly known as Jim Grant, was living proof of the biographical illusion. Five hundred pages made for a long book, but not a very long book, and even a very, very long book could never exhaustively account for sixty-five years (and counting) of a life well lived. I'd read my Jorge Luis Borges. I'd witnessed the heroic futility of Ireneo Funes as he sought desperately in 'Funes the Memorious' to enumerate the events of a single day or the contents of a single room, and had, in the end, died of pulmonary congestion – an ailment to which it seemed all too likely lifelong smoker Lee might one day succumb – suffocated beneath the asphyxiating weight of his memories, a mere nineteen years old, but 'monumental as bronze, more ancient than Egypt, anterior to the prophecies and the pyramids'. The epithet 'definitive' was habitually attached to biographies, but such a thing did not, and could not exist. I found consolation in this thought. *The Reacher Guy* would only ever be my contemporaneous interpretation of Lee Child's life, however resonant with his words; it was no more, and no less, than the book that I, at this point in time, had to write.

I felt that Lee himself would ask no more. For a book to have authenticity, he said, it had to be the work of a single mind; it must have a beating heart. 'Heart things' were a recurrent motif in his writing, prompted by the obscure cardiac crisis that had put him in Birmingham Children's Hospital for a month at the age of seven.

'I'm not complaining,' Lee remarked one time, explaining how he'd always felt unloved by his parents. 'Every little thing has turned me into what I am.' He had a way of saying simple things

Jim Grant, Transmission Controller - aka 'The Judge'. British Archive for Contemporary Writing, UEA.

James Dover Grant, aged two, with his grandfathers, Harry Dover Scrafton of South Shields and John 'No Middle Name' Grant of East Belfast. Family photo.

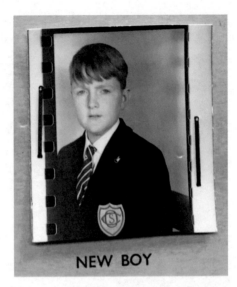

1965: Ten-year-old Jim Grant joins King Edward's School, Birmingham, founded by royal charter in 1552: 'At first, I was hungry for intellectual fodder.' KES Archive.

1974: 'All writers are wannabe rockstars.' From the private collection of Adrian Mudd, friend and wedding photographer of Jim Grant.

Seventeen, at home in Underwood Road, Handsworth Wood, reading the King Edward's Chronicle: 'I was in the middle of a big argument (by letter to the paper) with fellow pupil David Willetts, who later became a Tory minister.' Family photo.

February 2020: Lee Child - aka 'The Reacher Guy' - on the roof of Carmelite House, London, home of Hachette UK. Brian Aris for Little, Brown.

that stuck with you. Unsurprisingly, a lot of them were about writing books, or could be read that way. Books that worked, that did the job they were supposed to do and did it well, telling a good, satisfying story in the same way a restaurant is expected to serve up a good, satisfying dinner. These words were like 'how-to' manuals for me as I was writing, just as John D. MacDonald's Travis McGee series had been for Lee when he was starting out. I resolved to be alert to 'every little thing'. But I wouldn't over-think it. 'If you over-design you end up with a laundry list, and it comes out artificial.' A book was nothing but artifice, but somehow it had to come across as spontaneous, organic, like it could have grown on a tree.

A book was nothing but artifice, but somehow it had to come across as spontaneous, organic, like it could have grown on a tree

It would be easy to assume that this was the voice of experience speaking, and it was, but of eighteen years in commercial television, where there was a big audience and fast feedback, and you had ample opportunity to learn what audiences wanted, and how to please them. Lee had spent most of his time at Granada as a transmission controller, which was mostly technical, but with responsibility for trouble-shooting too, and the constant requirement to think on your feet. He liked having to take decisions and act on them and defend them. 'There were lots of vectors. We had to protect company revenue, comply with government regulations, consider public taste,

respect moral imperatives and accept responsibility.'
Controllers had to be on-the-spot responsive. 'If we
had news film about famine in Ethiopia, it didn't
feel right to be pushing Fray Bentos meat pies.' You
were 'thinking on behalf of the audience'. Almost
like being a writer of popular novels.

It was on the back of this, and thirty-six years of
reading, at the approximate rate of three hundred
books a year, that Jim Grant set out, on Monday
5 September 1994, to begin work on the thriller
that would, on 17 March 1997, be published in the
United States as *Killing Floor*.

'I'm not new to the entertainment media – I
worked in commercial television for nearly eighteen
years – but this is my first novel,' he wrote in his
first letter to Darley Anderson. 'I'm planning to
spend the next three years doing whatever it takes
to become a successful writer of commercial fiction.
I want to offer strong plots, tough characters,
realistic action, fresh perspectives – all written in a
way which is accessible to anybody, but with enough
inherent style to satisfy readers who look for more.'
It was a crystal-clear ambition, and not least of his
achievements is how faithfully he saw it through.

The working title was 'Bad Luck and Trouble'
(the list of possible alternatives batted around
over the next two and half years runs to several
handwritten pages), Lee Child was only a shadowy
figure in the ex-controller's mind, and Reacher had
not yet been named. That was one reason he chose
to write in the first person. Not only was it more

natural – from start to finish he saw himself as a storyteller, rather than a novelist – he didn't yet have a name for his hero. He was toying with 'Franklin' but wasn't convinced. It wasn't until 2272 words into chapter two that he wrote what now reads like a character blueprint – '"My name is Jack Reacher," I said. "No middle name. No address"' – little knowing how legendary those words would become.

I wasn't Lee Child. But we had things in common. Perhaps I wasn't about to write twenty-four stories about a single recurring character – 'the same but different', as he might say – but like him, I'd read plenty of books. And like him, I'd spent a good eighteen years on a previous career. I was the better typist, had taught myself to touch-type when I was doing my PhD, whereas he picked out all those hundreds of thousands of hundred-dollar words delicately with two index fingers. He wasn't bothered. 'I like going slow,' he wrote to me, when he was in the midst of writing *Blue Moon*. He recalled an essay by Umberto Eco on the importance of handwriting. It encouraged you to think through each sentence before you started writing. Lee had used a computer since partway into *Die Trying* but he still took the Eco approach. 'It makes for a cleaner first draft.' Computers, like digital film, bred a lazy extravagance, because you knew you could go back and fix it later. The speed of his typing was perfectly adapted to the speed of his creative brain, and if he went any faster his hands would trip up his head. Disciples would often quote his dictum: 'Don't get it right, get it

written.' But it was more 'Get it right as it's written'.
A waste-not want-not methodology in tune with his
frugal upbringing.

> **For him, it all started with first sentences. First
> sentences set the tone ... it was simply a case of
> following your nose, like a dog on the trail of a scent**

I decided to follow Lee's example. Not in typing
with two fingers, but in being guided by instinct.
For him, it all started with first sentences. First
sentences set the tone, and planted the first clues,
and after that it was simply a case of following your
nose, like a dog on the trail of a scent, as argued
by Carlo Ginzburg in his essay on the cynegetic
paradigm, or a hunter-gatherer pursuing a woolly
mammoth. First sentences were the way into any
book, but in Lee's case they opened the door to his
methodology, too: the more books he wrote, the
more Reacher began to think like a writer, and the
more effortlessly self-reflexive Lee's writing became.
His favourite of his own first sentences was the very
first one: 'I was arrested in Eno's diner.' Not least
for sentimental reasons. 'That was the beginning
of *Killing Floor*, and that was the beginning of the
whole thing,' he said. In interviews he claimed it
had never changed, but that wasn't strictly true.
The first sentence he wrote at his dining table,
using the pencil and paper he'd bought in his lunch
break from WHSmith at the Arndale Centre in
Manchester, was in fact: 'I had slept on the bus right
through the long haul from _____.' But this and
the next four lines had been almost immediately

crossed out, and crossed out again diagonally, and then he had got it just right and never looked back.

I found my first sentence in Otley, and from there my first chapter, which just as Lee had described, led on to the second, and then the third, until, by dint of following the threads, more than one hundred thousand words later I somehow reached what felt like an ending. It was 2017. I was in Harrogate, at the Theakston Old Peculier Crime Festival, where Lee was collecting a lifetime achievement award. I'd wanted to go to Otley ever since Lee had told me it was where his maternal grandparents had lived, and where he used to spend school holidays as a boy. Harry Dover Scrafton, a skilled naval draughtsman, whose middle name had been passed on to James Grant, was 'the only real human among my immediate ancestors', Lee wrote. 'Drank a little, gambled a little, smoked a lot.' When I told him I was going on a day trip he said simply: 'Make sure you visit the library. I read a lot of books there.' It was his grandmother, née Audrey Leider Scott, who had taken him there first. The librarian – the first person to whom I tentatively uttered the words 'Lee Child' and 'biography' in the same sentence, as if trying the idea out for size – was excited to learn that the Scraftons ('a strong name') had lived opposite her on Queen's Terrace. She dug out a selection of books on the old town, drawing attention to *This Little Town of Otley* by local author Harry Walker, the son and grandson of printers, which seemed to me auspicious. It wasn't until two years later that I discovered this was one of three books Lee had inherited from his grandma Scrafton, named Audrey, like his mother. The other two were *A Century of Thrillers: From Poe to Arlen*, and his own mother's *Collected Shakespeare* from her school days.

The week before Harrogate I had been in New York. I was there to attend ThrillerFest, at the Grand Hyatt Hotel on 42nd Street in midtown Manhattan, the year Lee was made ThrillerMaster. Since then I've grown accustomed to those branded neologisms, but at the time they sat awkwardly in my mouth. The biography was my excuse for collecting all manner of mementos: maybe I would make a scrapbook, as I invariably had when travelling as a child. My tickets to the Pre-Banquet Cocktail Party and the After Party in the Manhattan Ballroom, and my invitation to the Awards Banquet itself, where Lee would be serenaded by the thriller-writing duo of Parks and Palmer singing adapted versions of Beatles hits ('Eight Blurbs a Week' and 'Reacher Eating Pie in Diners'): everyone knew he'd always wanted to be a Beatle. Afterwards, Lee gave me the typed notes for his acceptance speech, which started like this:

> Book prizes - write speech?
> Jinx/disappointed/dork
> Agent/spouse/editor
> No excuse for me not to write a speech
> Feeling

In the top right corner of the page, in biro, he had jotted the following numbers:

$$122 = 144$$
$$212 = 441$$
$$132 = 169$$
$$312 = 961$$

I seem to recall some convoluted point about increase in membership since the International Thriller Writers association was founded in 2005, the same year he signed with Paramount and Tom Cruise; but more than that, I suspect he liked this elegant symmetry for its own sake, and also that if, like Reacher, he ever found himself handcuffed to a woman in the back of a van over several days and nights he would likely pass the time calculating big numbers in his head.

> **If, like Reacher, he ever found himself handcuffed to a woman ... over several days and nights he would likely pass the time calculating big numbers in his head**

This, I think, was when I was incurably bitten by the archive bug. At this point we were twenty-one years into Reacher's career, and twenty-three into Lee Child's: how many more such tantalising fragments might there be in existence?

The answer was: at least twenty-two boxes, roughly one for each year of his writing career. I know this because that's the number of boxes he dispatched to Norwich when, in 2018, he agreed to donate his papers to the British Archive for

Contemporary Writing at the University of East
Anglia. I wrote to the archivist for more detail.
This is what she wrote back:

> Archives are (or should be) universally
> measured in linear metres because boxes
> and shelves vary in size so much, so it's a
> way of doing a comparison.
>
> Lee's physical archive at UEA is 19 linear
> metres.
> Doris Lessing's is 85 linear metres but
> she never used a computer and also this
> represents her working life from approx
> 1960-2013.
> Raymond Chandler's archive at Oxford is
> 8.69 linear metres.
>
> But archives are also now being measured
> digitally in GBs or TBs. It would be
> interesting to analyse the diminishing
> physical vs the burgeoning digital.

Justine Mann would get on well with Jack Reacher.
Archivists in general, perhaps, not to mention
biographers. Reacher was 'a geek and a nerd in a
lot of ways', Lee confessed in 2016. 'But are you
going to tell him that?' Consider the debate around
the placing of the possessive apostrophe in *Killing
Floor*, or how the plot of *Without Fail* hinges on the
presence or absence of a hyphen, and that of *Gone
Tomorrow* on the niceties of spelling. Reacher may

not have shamelessly surrendered to his nerdy side until his twenty-third outing, *Past Tense*, when the pretext of researching his own genealogy (was this a biographer's influence at work?) gave him permission to hang out in the library, but it was built in from the very beginning. It was not for nothing that Reacher had received a European education, was well versed in Latin and Greek, and did not shy away from the occasional reference to Balzac, Proust or even Marcuse. The great King Edward's School in Birmingham would be proud to claim him as one of their own.

I loved the weeks, or months, that I spent in the archive, channelling my inner Reacher nerd. But I was glad that the opportunity had arisen relatively late in the process. Otherwise I might, like Funes, have risked asphyxiation under the weight of those twenty-two boxes. The detail was potentially infinite, and dangerously absorbing. The big-picture overview was instructive too, describing a pleasing narrative arc. Earlier boxes, dating from the late 1990s, are heavy with densely annotated manuscripts and correspondence between writer and editors. In the middle period, letters from fans are beginning to stack up. So too the accolades and awards. Later boxes are equally weighty, but their contents increasingly repetitive. Two genres predominate: blurb requests (and effusive thank-you notes) from publishers and writers; and letters about Cruise.

Regardless of content, the sheer quantity of words just kept on multiplying. Well beyond the approximately two and a half million devoted by

Lee to Reacher himself. But so too did the numbers (and I don't just mean contracts and royalty statements).

Sure enough, there were pages of painstaking calculations, almost like Jim Grant was missing school. Only a few have to do with plot (these examples all relate to *Killing Floor*):

A dollar bill weighs 0.94 gram ($\approx$ 1)
1064 dollars = 2.2 pounds
1,083,345 dollars = 1 ton
1 pound of single dollar bills = $480
1 ton of single dollar bills = approx $1 million
30 dollars = 1 oz
$480 = 1 lb
airconditioner box = ? 200 lbs = $96,000

Most are obsessively concerned with the internal economy of the text. A 'schedule' lists page counts for each chapter across different drafts. There is a comparison of his own pen draft with books by James Patterson and Patricia Cornwell: overall number of pages, number of lines per page and number of characters per line. A note reads '257 words per page (on my draft)'. On the facing page Lee has written:

What the writer needs is a sixty-two character line
What this page needs is a line of sixty-two characters
What this page needs are lines of sixty-two characters each
* What these lines need are lengths of sixty-two characters each

Patterson's lines were typically 63 characters long. Lee notes that Grisham's *The Firm* has 62 characters x 40 lines, whereas his 'Bad Luck and Trouble' ('Bad' for short) has 79 characters x 28 lines. He is happy with the ratios. He tots up the total number of letters in 189 words (ranging between 1 and 13 characters in length) and calculates an average word length of 4.15 characters – 'call it 4'. He concludes: 'Aim for 472 pages or more of my m/s.'

'The work you put in was epic,' I wrote to him after my first week. 'I know,' he answered. 'Unimaginable now. Got very lazy'

'The work you put in was epic,' I wrote to him after my first week. 'I know,' he answered. 'Unimaginable now. Got very lazy.'

I was reminded of his old form master: 'Only his own efforts can ensure success.' But James Dover Grant CBE didn't really care what the masters thought. They were the educational equivalent of newspaper critics. The motivational words he harked back to came from one of his Sixth-Form contemporaries, S. D. 'Sid' Jones. Sid was only a middling rugby player, but had once given a terrific team talk that had stuck with Jim forever.

'My motto,' Lee wrote to me, quoting Sid: 'I can't grow any more talent, but I can out-work you.'

'It's something they teach you in the army,' said Reacher in *Blue Moon*. The only thing under your direct control, the hero went on – and he might as well have been speaking of his creator – is how hard you work. In other words, if you really buckle down today, and you get the intelligence, the planning, and the execution each a hundred percent exactly correct, then you are bound to prevail.

Heather Martin's The Reacher Guy:
The Authorised Biography of Lee Child
is out now from Constable at Little, Brown 🄷

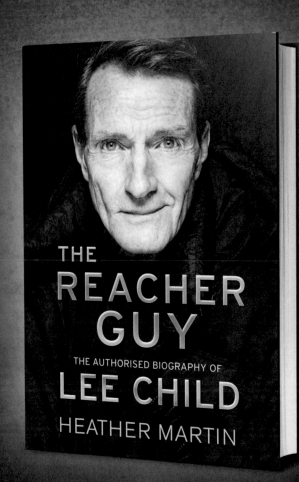

Three people lost

their lives

by Sahanika Ratnayake

This image was originally posted to Flickr by ChiralJon and has been converted to greyscale

On the evening of the 29th of November, I am on the train home from London when Ben abruptly adds me to a Whatsapp group titled 'News'. Ben types for a long time and I am considering asking if this is his way of announcing that his partner is pregnant when the message comes through. Ben tells us not to worry. He says that the knife attack on London Bridge, currently being reported on the news, actually began earlier, at a nearby event that he was attending at Fishmongers' Hall. He is safe but some of his friends are hurt. He says he does not want to talk but asks that we hold him in our thoughts and prayers. This is exactly the sort of request Ben would make.

It is the first I've heard anything about a knife attack. I have not read the news because I have been teaching all day. I cannot fathom what sort of event Ben would have been attending at Fishmongers' Hall on a Friday afternoon during *term time. The word terrorist gets used immediately in the coverage and my heart sinks. Terrorism had been a recurring theme of that year, and each time I had found myself hoping that it would not turn out to be a brown Muslim man.*

It is only when I get home that the news starts saying the attack began at a University of Cambridge conference celebrating the five-year anniversary of the Learning Together program.

On one of our first trips to prison, Ben tells us that the flat monotony of the landscape that we are driving through resulted from the draining of the Fens, an area of marshland in Cambridgeshire that was once underwater. What we are looking at is essentially sea floor. Ben is the sort of person who speaks in fully formed paragraphs, his speech dotted with oddly specific historical anecdotes. He mentions that one of the early investors in the drainage project was a 'Potato Baron' interested in new farming land for his vast potato empire. We spend the rest of the trip laughing about carrot barons and soy bean barons.

HMP Whitemoor, a Category A men's prison, is located in the Fenlands, near the town of March. I made this journey every week for several months, as a group facilitator for the Learning Together program. Learning Together brings undergraduates into prisons to learn alongside prison students. There are a number of educational activities that fall under the umbrella of Learning Together, from reading groups to courses on everything from Law to French Literature. I was part of a course called 'Good Life and Good Society'. Each session began with a lecture by a professor from Cambridge University followed by discussions in small groups, one of which I facilitated.

I am terrified that the attacker might be someone I know. Realistically this can't be right, because I saw everyone in Whitemoor mere months ago and they could not have been released in the meantime. But I scour the news looking for a picture. When I finally find one, I try to imagine it in various permutations: without the beard, thinner, fatter, smiling. Finally I relax, reassured that I have never met this particular brown Muslim man.

I am terrified that the attacker might be someone I know. Realistically this can't be right ... but I scour the news looking for a picture

Facilitating a group discussion in prison is no different from teaching in general. I worry about the same things, obsessively. I worry about how to get certain students to talk more and others to talk less. I try desperately to stop John from telling meandering stories about his nights out in Glasgow, which leave us laughing but completely off track. I attempt to lure Ahmed into speaking. He only opens up, truly, when he is talking about his son. I worry, in turn, that the material is too difficult or not stimulating enough. I suspect that Gary would have enjoyed university – I am proved right when I read his essay at the end of the course and find myself thinking that of my students, he is the best suited for philosophy. He is the only one who openly challenges the material. This is the wild egalitarianism of philosophy that I love. You can never be too famous, too clever or too well-established to be wrong; even a prisoner may disagree with Aristotle.

I worry about the same things, but with added salt. I worry about what it means when it is the Whitemoor students that are not speaking. Their silence embodies a complex shyness to do with lost educational opportunities and shame. I worry when the Cambridge students listen, riveted, when the topic turns to prison. It is voyeuristic but it seems monstrous to interrupt and redirect to the readings; I cannot pretend that I am not also fascinated.

The sessions are hit and miss: Aristotle early on is popular, the one on the methodology of anthropology, disastrous. Something shifts when we have the session on criminology. Alison Liebling lectures on trust in prisons. She has worked in Whitemoor before and seems to know most of the people in the room. Suddenly, the Whitemoor students are voluble with stories of complicated interactions with prison guards and loved ones. Someone asks how trust is possible when, by the time they get to prison, they have watched their friends and family testify against them in court. Gary tells us of the time he spent in isolation, how there were years when he did not get to see the sky. I do not know what to say. I relinquish control over the discussion. This time, the Whitemoor students have no trouble speaking and those of us from Cambridge listen silently, the reading forgotten.

That night, after the session on trust, I went to the pub. I do not normally drink alone. I am angry, I feel cheated by my profession. Nothing I have ever read or learned in my many years of studying philosophy gives me comfort, or even comprehension in this moment. I began the course wondering idly about moral terms, how I was to reconcile the badness of the act, murder, terrorism, what have you, with the person who had committed it. A person who I could find funny, or hospitable, or interested in the same obscure Dracula remakes. The criminologists and the ordinands that populate the course seem far better equipped to navigate this distinction, largely because they do not seem to make it in the first place. It occurs to me that when I have needed solace in the past, I have read Ecclesiastes, not moral philosophy, and certainly not moral philosophy in the analytic tradition, of which I am a part. Moral philosophers seem to be children quibbling over the most useless of words – 'permissible', 'blameworthy', 'superorgarative' – determined to stick the peeling labels of obscure moral terms onto phenomena that barely resemble the agony of lived experience.

I drank, watched the moon over the river, and wondered if the cost of taking a life was commensurable with being deprived a view of the sky.

Once it becomes clear that I do not know the attacker, I panic about who was hurt. I start checking the social media of people who were likely to be present. Ruth Armstrong and Amy Ludlow, the founders of Learning Together, had to be there. Their Twitter accounts have been locked down,

which I find promising – someone had to change the account
settings, so they are likely to be unharmed. I think of Alice
next, Alice who was one of the coordinators for my course.
She has not posted on Twitter since yesterday. I am about
to message her when I realise her number has been somehow
replaced with a different Alice's since the course ended. I send
an email and a flurry of messages to other Learning Together
friends, asking for her number.

Shortly after Alice replies, the papers start saying that
Jack is dead.

I drank, watched the moon over the river, and wondered if the cost of taking a life was commensurable with being deprived a view of the sky

I am in Alice's office, telling her the worst thing I
have ever done. It is the sort of thing you inevitably
end up doing, when you are the sort of person who
reaches too readily for anger. When you reach for
anger first. After I finish, I ask jokingly whether
she is going to run away. Alice is not so stupid as to
think this is actually a joke. She conducts interviews
for a living. Her research is on men convicted of sex
offences, a crime that carries with it a great deal of
stigma, even for the prison system. She is an expert
on getting the reluctant to talk. She would normally
pause here. Alice's speech is punctuated with
pauses, sometimes in the middle of sentences. But
today she responds, unhesitatingly with the same
calculated flippancy, 'Well, I am still here aren't I?'

I am not entirely sure how we ended up at
my confession. I had asked to meet with her to

talk about some strange dynamics between my Whitemoor students that I wasn't sure how to manage. The conversation was typical of those that happen within Learning Together, meandering between various topics and our own lives. We had somehow talked about everything from philosophical pedagogy, power in prisons, to moral language and culpability. Alice tells me that the people who are involved in Learning Together fall roughly into two camps on the question of culpability. People who believe that once an offence has been committed and the punishment doled out, there was nothing more to be thought about it, morally speaking. Then there were those who looked at those convicted of crimes and thought, 'There but for the grace of God'.

I have heard that particular cry multiple times. It is the noise that mothers make, falling to their knees, when their children have died in a bus bomb

When Alice interviews me after the course is over, I will insist she turn the recorder back on so I can tell her that Learning Together gave me something that no amount of therapy, reflection, so-called self-acceptance and time could. I had learnt to make peace with the things I had done, by quietly taking my place amongst other people.

We fell out towards the end of the course. I had sent my apologies for the end-of-course celebration, a graduation of sorts, held at the end of April 2019. Alice responded by urging me to reconsider and I replied furiously to her email, baffled that anyone could think it was appropriate to attend a celebration when both the countries that I called 'mine' had just been hit by the biggest terrorist attacks in their history.

The vigil marking Jack's death is held at the Cambridge Guildhall on the Monday morning following his death. What most of us will remember from that day were the sounds of agony his girlfriend would make periodically, her grief hitting her in waves.

Beth, the other coordinator for the course, will later refer to this as the wail of grief, instantly identifiable to anyone who has encountered loss. For me, this is the wail of suicide bombing. When I was a teenager, my parents did something very peculiar for immigrants – they went back. They abandoned New Zealand, their adopted country and returned to Sri Lanka. I have heard that particular cry multiple times. It is the noise that mothers make, falling to their knees, when their children have died in a bus bomb.

In the face of such very private, personal grief, I feel out of place. I barely knew Jack. I had spoken to him briefly, but for the most part, he was a person who sent me administrative emails and hovered at the edges of our sessions in Whitemoor. Everything I know of Saskia, whose vigil is happening on the other side of the city centre, I learnt from the news alongside the news of her death. I attend Jack's vigil, numbly because I do not know what else to do. Even worse, I am here because I want to confirm with my own eyes that my friends are not hurt. The names of the injured have been suppressed, so I am reduced to crossing people's names off in my head when I see them in the crowd. My eyes meet those of one of the Criminology receptionists, and she nods slightly. I realise I am not the only one silently crossing off names.

*Ruth and Amy are dressed inappropriately for such a
sombre occasion, which I find comforting. Amy is wearing
a bright red coat and Ruth, in a textured hoodie and jeans,
looks, as always, impossibly fashionable. As I hug them,
they whisper 'sorry' in a way that makes me think they are
apologising, instead of comforting me for my loss. If Jack's
death has the sharp rebuke of a Greek tragedy, a reminder
that you can never be too young or clever or beautiful to die,
Ruth and Amy's story seems no less tragic. A warning about
the fragility of things, that even the most tenderly built life's
work can one day sit in pieces around your feet.*

*I clutch Ben's coat during the moment of silence, as
I clutch Alice when I finally find her in the crowd. I am
convinced that they cannot die if I have them in my grip.*

The mosque shootings in Christchurch followed
by the Easter bombings in Sri Lanka were a one-
two punch. They were two sides of the same coin.
Both targeted religious institutions and involved
extremism, extremism of different stripes, but
extremism nonetheless. One was said to be a
response to the other; I am still not sure what
to make of that. New Zealand, a country where
nothing much ever happens, let alone anything bad,
seemed to lose its innocence overnight. It became
like anywhere else, a place that could harbour
hatred. In Sri Lanka, which did not have much
innocence to begin with, the attack harkened back
to the civil war, though the country had not seen
anything of this nature. Whilst the first destroyed
me, the second struck me as the cruellest – to
opportunistically take from those who had so

little, not even innocence, to begin with. I felt as
if someone had wrenched my childhood from my
chest and viciously stomped on it. Ecclesiastes no
longer braced me and I turned to Job instead. I took
a great number of sad baths over many months. I
did not know how to reconcile myself to a world
where people were killed as they prayed.

**I took a great number of sad baths over many
months. I did not know how to reconcile myself
to a world where people were killed as they prayed**

When we return to prison for one last visit,
having apologised for missing the end-of-term
celebration, I find myself telling Gary about the
Easter bombings. He describes them as 'evil', which
shocks me. I cannot recall ever encountering this
word in conversation, as an adjective available to
anyone. Even now, this is a word whose contours I
explore with my fingertips. By now, I have learnt
that it matters who holds a position, who uses a
word. In philosophy we pretend, on pain of fallacy,
that this is not so. We act as if it is the argument
that matters, not the one who espouses it. I have
learnt otherwise from John who I used to harangue
every week. No matter what the topic was, John
would refuse to hold any definite view on it,
cheerfully exclaiming, 'Ah well, live and let live, I
say'. During a session on anger and justice, he tells
us how angry he is at himself, for what he has done
and the pain he has caused. It proved impossible to
bring him back to the reading on moral emotions.
Privately, he tells me that this is why he has no

thoughts on any of these topics that I keep trying to bait him with. 'Who am I to say how someone else should live?', he asks, and I am ashamed for believing his moral relativism to be glib, rather than hard won. And so when Gary uses the word 'evil', it means something to me. It means something to hear it spoken out loud, in this place, by a Muslim. By someone who knows something about the outer edges of human experience.

———

In the weeks following everything, I become obsessed with learning German vocabulary, something I was far too lazy to do when I was actively taking German classes. I start going to Quaker meetings. Ben is a Quaker, and I diligently try to honour his request by trying to hold him in my thoughts during the silent worship every Sunday. I sneak out immediately after, I cannot bear to talk to anyone over tea and cake. It is as if I do not know how to paste familiar words onto the world. I do not know how to respond with anything other than silence.

An old friend gets back in touch and, after listening to the whole tale, says casually, 'And I suppose, you are angry about it all'

An old friend gets back in touch and, after listening to the whole tale, says casually, 'And I suppose, you are angry about it all'. I realise to my surprise that I hold no anger towards Usman and never have. The question reminds me of something Alice tells me, when we meet again a few days after Jack's memorial. When she was being barraged with questions about what happened, but unable to answer them as it was an ongoing investigation, she had been advised by Ruth and Amy to say only that three people had been killed. It takes me a moment to understand the significance of what she has said. For Ruth and Amy, all the tragedy of the situation was condensed into the fact that three young people lost their lives.

I am a person who obsesses over words. I do not know if it is a professional hazard, or the reason I ended up with this profession in the first place. In either case, I will wonder about the differences, if there are any, between these sentences, for some time:

A terrorist killed two people.

One person, who most likely, would have once shared tea and cake with the others, killed them.

One person killed two others.

Three people were killed.

Three people lost their lives. ◧

Short online creative writing courses

Make 2021 your writing year — book now for January!

- Study online at any time from the comfort of home
- Fully tutored, receive individual feedback on your work
- Small, friendly groups — 15 students max
- Beginner and intermediate levels available
- Co-designed with the University of East Anglia

Beginning 25 January 2021 – book soon!

nationalcentreforwriting.org.uk/creative-writing-online/

'The materials were excellent and the tutor feedback was so helpful. I feel I have learned such a lot and my writing has definitely improved as a result.'

Lisa Tippings, Start Writing Creative Non-Fiction

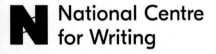

HOME

by Tom Price

I woke up on the floor outside. I was curled in a ball on the patio, with no shirt or shoes, no socks and no idea of what had happened. It was light and warm, but I had no clue what time it was.

My parents were abroad and I'd invited friends over the previous night. We drank and smoked and made our way into town. We visited the usual pubs and clubs: O'Neill's, Cody's, The Church. At The Roof, the most popular place for our crowd to end up, I bought two double-vodka Red Bulls and poured them into a pint glass, making what had come to be known locally as a Lazy

Boy (staff were not allowed to serve quadruples
in a single container, so we had to do it this way).
In the process, I covered my shirt in splashes of
sticky brown liquid, nodding to acquaintances
across the bar as I wiped my hands on my jeans.
The dancefloor heaved with bodies, twisting and
throbbing below the flashing blue lights. Out in the
garden, I chatted to people I went to school with,
telling stories, and chain-smoking. When I ran out
of cigarettes, I scanned the crowd for someone I felt
comfortable sponging off — a friend who wasn't
bothered, or an acquaintance whose judgement
would have little effect on me. I was forever
pinching cigarettes.

Over the years, smoking had come to represent
something significant in my life. It helped me make
friends at school, providing valuable common
ground. We'd meet at the bus station and often
share one cigarette between three — during which
time we'd talk about all sorts. Smoking facilitated
communication and, in a place where everyone
was encouraged to follow the path and do the right
thing, it was a chance to do the wrong thing as a
group; to come together and challenge authority.
There was something comforting and exhilarating
in this. When we left wherever we were in order
to smoke, there was nothing to do but talk. If the
conversation was good, we'd have another, then
another. I often found that the better the night,
the more I stank in the morning, the more phlegm
there was congealed in my throat, the more yellow
tar staining my fingers.

On this occasion, I was smoking with a group of boys I knew reasonably well; we'd spent time playing football together and hanging out in the fields, but they weren't good friends as such. A few months earlier, I'd been back to one of their houses for a party after town and got so drunk I fell full-length into the fish pond in the garden. I'd had to borrow clothes while mine dried in the machine. I had been worried about bumping into them ever since — such instances always caused me anxiety afterwards. Under the influence, however, I was able to laugh it off. As it turned out, they thought it was hilarious. They said I was nuts.

A few months earlier, I'd been back to one of their houses for a party after town and got so drunk I fell full-length into the fish pond in the garden

We sat at a table in the corner and smoked for ages, every now and then dipping our fingers into small resealable bags, rubbing dabs of MDMA over our gums. I spoke passionately about the music I'd gotten into, spluttering on about Boards of Canada, Deerhunter and Aphex Twin, as if I'd graduated from the punk and hardcore we'd grown up on. A couple of the boys I'd arrived with drifted around the conversation. It was always like this with my closest friends: we'd spend most of the night together, then disperse towards closing time, filtering off into different groups, expanding our horizons. They watched me talk for a few minutes and passed glances between them. They found my enthusiasm for bands, books and films laughable, sometimes embarrassing. It wasn't so much the subject matter, but the way I spoke about these things, with gushing authority. Everything was amazing. And I heard too little of what others had to say.

Soon enough, we were ushered into the street by a troop of red-faced, muscle-bound bouncers. We gathered in clusters outside the kebab shops and smoked some more. A police van was pulled up nearby, because this was where fights usually happened. One of the boys I'd been sat with invited me back to his house for another party. I joined a queue and ordered chips and spicy battered mushrooms, covered them in mayonnaise and chilli sauce and hung around, waiting for a minibus to ship us out to the countryside.

The night dissolved into waves the colour of sweaty clothes and pallid flesh. I had food on my face and my lips were burning from the chilli. A taxi stopped in the distance and Will led the way to the bottom of Station Hill. I sat next to Amy, who I'd met at a festival in Newquay earlier that summer. She was really nice. I sobered up enough to hold a conversation; we spoke about the trip to Cornwall, friends we had in common, our plans for the coming year.

We left the town centre and joined the main road to the coast. We passed a cheap spa hotel and a drug dealer's mansion, then crossed the bridge, verdure bursting from the dark riverbanks. We turned left into a village and drove up a steep hill to a house I'd never seen before, surrounded by woods and fields. I remember little of its exterior.

My conversation with Amy continued in a bedroom on the top floor, where four or five of us smoked joints and played American punk CDs. More cars pulled into the drive and the music below shook the floorboards. Somehow, we got to talking about our grandfathers, who had both died of Alzheimer's. We held hands for a short time. My palm was sweating. She stood up and went downstairs.

In the bathroom, I locked the door. I seem to recall a beige or mustard finish and a strong scent of lavender, like that of my grandparents' house near Tewkesbury. There were photos from family holidays on the walls and rolls of toilet paper stacked in neat piles. I spat in the sink and looked at myself in the mirror: the reddish-brown, spiked fringe, hairline already receding at the edges; slim, angular face, long, flushed and lightly freckled; steep forehead, butt of so many jokes. I cared a great deal about my appearance. Whenever I caught sight of my reflection, I would lift my eyebrows in order to shorten the distance between them and my hair, creating rows of grotesque creases instead. *Fuck it.* I swigged from a can of flat, flavourless lager and brushed my hair forward with my hands. Had I said something to put Amy off? Or had the lighting revealed too much detail? I threw water on my cheeks and stooped to use the toilet. For some reason, I dragged the back of my hand across the shower curtain on the way out.

Back in the bedroom, I sat down to chat to Will, Scampy and two lads I hadn't met before, farmers from a nearby village. Despite the pot, which usually made me stew in a state of quiet paranoia, I was talking freely and with confidence – the MDMA had continued to flow. I was making them laugh. Before long, I was talking about the two weeks' jury service I'd had to do. It was a case of serious child abuse and the accused was closely related to someone moderately famous. As such, the judge stressed how important it was not to disclose any of the details of the trial outside the courtroom. I'd stuck to this guidance, not sharing a scrap of information with anyone, not even my parents; now, all of a sudden, here I was divulging it all to two acquaintances and a couple of strangers. They hung on every word as I gave names, locations, witness testimony and a condensed version of the judge's summary. When I think of this now, I picture myself spitting and frothing at the mouth.

He reached into his pocket. Do you boys fancy a pill by any chance? A wave of excitement crashed over me

It was shocking, I've never heard anything like it, I explained. *It's really affected me.*

I bet. One of them seemed particularly interested, but he might have been taking the piss.

I've got fuck all faith in our justice system now. A couple of big characters on the jury take control and decide the verdict. It's crazy.

Fuck. I'd love to do it – proper interesting. He reached into his pocket. *Do you boys fancy a pill by any chance?* A wave of excitement crashed over me. *They take a while to get going,* he warned, *but they're pretty good.*

We swallowed the swollen pink tablets, stamped with images of freakish cartoon characters, and joined the others in the living room downstairs. It was dark. Some people were dancing, but most were sat at a large dining table, rolling cigarettes and downing shots of whisky. It had the air of a séance. We filled the vacant seats and a drinking game soon began, led by another lad I'd never met before. He seemed huge, his broad shoulders hunched and his face pockmarked with acne scars. I don't recall how, but at some point the bag of ecstasy appeared on the table and became a feature of the game. I was offered the choice of three upturned cups, below which was either a shot, a pill, or the option to nominate someone else. I looked at the rows of wonky smiles and half-closed eyes, blurred and twitching. I lifted the cup: a pink tablet. Never one to say no, I took it in my fingers and, despite a flurry of nerves, washed it down with a sip of warm lager. The first pill hadn't kicked in yet.

Most were sat at a large dining table, rolling cigarettes and downing shots of whisky. It had the air of a séance. We filled the vacant seats and a drinking game soon began

In no time at all, the cups completed another circuit and were placed in front of me again. I raised the one in the middle and found more ecstasy. The boy whose turn it was before mine had refused to take a second pill, but this was not an option I would consider, despite it being my third. It was as if I had something to prove, and this sort of behaviour would do it – some bizarre expression of bravery: machismo born of booze and insecurity.

I took the pill and tipped over the two remaining cups, drinking the whisky for good measure. Laughter rippled around the table and I heard someone say I was mental, which, at that moment, pleased me. More rounds followed.

This is the last portion of the night I remember with any clarity. I see flashes of myself – like a broken film reel – sitting on the kitchen counter talking shit to Will, his eyes rolling in the back of his head. There were further trips to the bathroom, where I splashed more water on my face, my body boiling beneath my skin. The sun rose over the house and there was a discussion about how to get me home. I was in the garden, writhing around in a patch of dried mud, winding up the family dog – a golden Labrador, I think. I don't know if I was still wearing a shirt at this point or not. A small crowd had formed around me, watching with expressions of amusement mixed with disgust. I caught sight of Amy; she looked repulsed.

I love dogs, I kept repeating, before the boy whose home it was came and led his pet away.

All of sudden, I was buying cigarettes in the shop by the school, then stumbling topless past the maths block and on between the portakabins where they taught languages. And then we are back to the patio flagstones, where I woke up stomach churning and the tendons in my jaw ablaze. My phone, keys and wallet were gone, as well as my shirt and shoes. I got up and walked barefoot onto the lawn, where, as a child, I scored goals and tries, dreaming of who I might one day become.

I wandered back and forth around the house, between the gardens, in a fugue state. I was still fucked. I smoked cigarettes in plain view of our neighbour, who was cutting the grass. He called a few words over the wall, and I replied with nonsense. I have no idea how long this went on for – it was as if I were dreaming, totally apart from any usual flow.

As I walked from the patio to the front porch, onto the drive and down to the beech trees, a kind of devastation crept upon me. Despite the interior of my childhood home being physically inaccessible, the past – my entire history – and the present had never before felt so entwined. I saw my tiny body sprawled lengthways across a branch, a cuddly toy hanging from my jaws. I saw my brother, Rob, bleeding on the floor, the back of his head gashed open and our friend's arms covered in blood. I saw that same friend whipping my bare back with bamboo in the shed at Rob's command. In the living room, through the sliding doors, we were sat at my father's feet as he peeled an orange, a newspaper splayed open on his lap, handing us juicy segments in turn and stroking our heads. There was a Ninja Turtle cake on the counter in the kitchen, my schoolmates sat around with grease on their smiling mouths – this is straight from a photograph. I saw myself sobbing into my pillow when my father, as a solution to my insomnia, sent me to bed at six o'clock; my brother and our neighbours still playing in the next room.

These visions were deeply unsettling. I had no watch or other means of telling the time, so at some point – when it finally occurred to me to do so – I peered in through the kitchen window at the clock on the cooker: 7.15. Jesus, I could only have been home an hour or so. Then it dawned on me: I'd spent the entire afternoon outside the house, strolling around like this. The realisation rocked me to my core – there was something in it about the stability of my existence, my place in the world. It was evening now and Rob had not come home. Was he coming back at all tonight? How was I going to get in? I had to collect my parents from the airport the following day. This was ridiculous. My mouth was bone dry, and the comedown was really starting to kick in.

What would the neighbours think? They had watched me grow into this. Any suspicions they had that I was heading for trouble were now confirmed

I had some loose change in my pocket, so I walked to the phone box at the top of the street. I called Rob's mobile three times, but it was off. Jason, my older brother, who lived around the corner, was away, and James, the eldest, was somewhat apart from the family at this point, and I couldn't remember his number. I walked back as quickly as possible, mortified by the fact I was still half naked and dishevelled, a staggering mess. What would the neighbours think? They had watched me grow into this. Any suspicions they had that I was heading for trouble were now confirmed. I was so thirsty. My hands trembled and I was struggling to withstand huge waves of nausea.

I pressed my face back up against the kitchen window. James's old number was written on the notice board, but had he kept it when he moved house? I repeated the combination over and over in my mind as I tried, unsuccessfully, to piss in the compost, my prostate searing with a too-familiar pain. I passed the car Dad had recently bought me – a silver Peugeot – and, with no hope whatsoever, reached out to try the handle. It clicked open. Finally, a bit of luck. I searched the contents of the boot and found a jumper, a pair of flip flops and a small, weeks-old bottle of water, which I had the wherewithal to sip with moderation. I walked back to the phone box, a little more confidently, and tried the number: the line was dead. I had friends nearby, but I couldn't face them, let alone their parents.

I recalled a drive to football training, when my father told me how happy he'd been in his first marriage, and how unhappy he was now

I sat on the doorstep, the light fading now, and wondered when it was my mother had withdrawn into herself. Had she always spent long hours apart from us, in the separate, smaller living room? At what point did Dad disappear into his work, leaving me to fend off my brother alone? There were plenty of happy memories stored up within the walls of this house, but there was so much sadness and anger too, so much dissatisfaction. Maybe it was just me. I recalled a drive to football training, when my father told me how happy he'd been in his first marriage, and how unhappy he was now. He and my mother always fought – it was incessant. And why couldn't me and Rob get on like his first two boys? He asked how I'd feel if he moved out. *I wouldn't mind*, I said. I was too young for this and the other conversations like it.

Richard, who lived next door, called over to me: Still no one home?

I flushed red. *Not yet*. I couldn't remember what I'd said to him earlier.

Why don't you come in, have something to eat? It looked as if he was having a party, cars pulled up on the drive.

Thanks Richard, but Rob's on his way back now – he'll be here soon.

OK, if you're sure. He went inside.

I stepped over to the Peugeot and climbed into the front seat. I pushed it right back and let my thoughts stray, to where everything I knew felt strange and unfamiliar, violent. Old forgotten scenes sprung up from nowhere and attacked my senses, making me long to return to the innocence of childhood or, better still, to flee to somewhere far away, where I could put all of this behind me. I thought back over the past twenty-four hours and pretended – involuntarily and quick as a flash – to put a gun in my mouth and pull the trigger.

I sat up, rubbed my eyes and turned the radio on. I listened to a documentary about Pavarotti, then switched to Classic FM. This was not like me. I dipped in and out of sleep for a while, each time waking desperate for another swig of water.

I dreamt of slugs and millipedes wriggling in beds of soil, the darkness in the fields behind the house. Trees in the garden, which creaked in the wind and knew me so well. Eels I'd caught at the bend in the river and cut into chunks to use as bait.

Cold crept into my bones and my lips were raw — I'd licked a layer of skin clean off. I finished the water, tucked my knees under my jumper, and shivered until morning.

———

I woke up so parched I began to panic. My mouth was swollen with cold sores and my gums were covered in ulcers. I hadn't eaten anything for nearly thirty hours and felt even more hungover than the previous night. The car battery had died, so time was once again a mystery. I stumbled to the kitchen window and peered in at the cooker: 10.00. I was due to pick up my parents in three hours. I surveyed the house for open windows, but it was pointless. What I really needed was water.

Thirty minutes later, Richard came into the garden with a pile of washing for the line. I leaned over the wall and called to him in a whisper.

Sorry to bother you, Richard. I cleared my throat. *I couldn't get something to drink, could I? I'm still locked out.*

Oh my God. He looked genuinely concerned. He rushed inside and came back almost immediately with a litre bottle of orange squash and a KitKat. *Why didn't you come and tell us?*

I thought Rob was on his way back. I was waiting and then fell asleep in the car. I'm fine, just a bit thirsty. I downed two thirds of the bottle, my hand shaking uncontrollably.

Have you tried Linda for a key?

Linda came to clean twice a week. She lived about two-hundred yards on from the phone box and most definitely did have a key.

Jesus Christ, I didn't even think. I couldn't believe it hadn't occurred to me.

Come on, I'll give you a lift.

I became conscious of my own stench: a foul blend of stale tobacco, alcohol, probably garlic, and a mouth that had been through hell

He wouldn't take no for an answer, and I was too exhausted to argue. Sat on the passenger side of his plush four-by-four – a newer version of the one I'd washed for money years before – I became conscious of my own stench: a foul blend of stale tobacco, alcohol, probably garlic, and a mouth that had been through hell, not to mention the sweat reeking under my arms. I tried not to touch the leather upholstery. We didn't say much – I just kept thanking him. He told me to stop.

When, at last, I turned the key, savouring the series of clicks that accompanied the full rotation, I almost cried. I collapsed onto my front, rolling around on the carpet, thrusting my limbs up and down as if to make snow angels. Never in my life had the smell of home been so sweet. I crawled to the sofa and turned on the television, dozing for a while, before climbing the stairs to take a shower. As I washed away the layers of grime, I told myself that what had happened was simply another funny story. It was normal for people my age to get into a few scrapes. My friends would love it; my parents would, too – if I told it right. I got dressed and went downstairs. I ate an apple in the kitchen, drank pints of cold water and set off in my mother's car for the airport.

They were worried at first, by the sight of my bulbous lips, but when I explained my ordeal – a grin spread across my face, leading with the line, *You won't believe the two days I've had* – my mum shook her head and broke into that wheezing laugh. *That's terrible.* She always enjoyed it when I distilled the humour from this sort of thing – the sanitised version, of course. There was no mention of drugs or excessive drinking. I just focussed on my own misfortune and made it all sound pretty innocuous, which was a comfort to me, too. Dad stayed quiet. He was probably thinking about something else altogether. **H**

LONDON LIT LAB

Online writing courses

Sign up for a London Lit Lab course in 2021. We offer online courses for all writers, from beginners to advanced.

Topics include: creative nonfiction, hybrid writing, folklore and fairy tales, fantastic and literary fiction, memoir, flash fiction, queer writing, YA and writing for young people.

Join our community and nurture your talent in a supportive environment with like-minded people, where writers teach writers.

Find out more about our courses, plus mentoring and critiquing services, at **www.londonlitlab.co.uk**

Or get in touch at **info@londonlitlab.co.uk** for a chat.

'Lily and Zoe offer teaching and coaching at the highest level. Their workshops have a reputation for encouraging excellence and creativity in a supportive environment. I am always recommending them.'
Julia Bell, Course Convenor, MA Creative Writing, Birkbeck.

BIG HUGS AND KISSES

by
Alice
Jolly

It was raining that day and it rained then for many days afterwards – or that's how I remember it anyway. And there I was driving back after dropping the children at school. Muddy water splashed up from the road, the windscreen wipers flicked and squeaked, the sky was gathering on the horizon, grey and hostile.

He – or it – was there on the side of the road. The first thing I saw was a tiny leg, pale grey and very long, pathetically splayed up the side of the verge. What? What? That leg must be part of a toy, I told myself. Or maybe a doll, which had fallen from a passing car and now lay in the mud.

Driving back the next time, I slowed down so that I could see it more clearly. The toy was wearing a small, tight-fitting red jacket and I'm sure that I saw ears, rabbit ears. After that I started to dread driving that way. The sight of this tiny thing on the side of the road upset me. I imagined it to be a toy rabbit, with extraordinarily long legs, and long ears as well. I thought of the Beatrix Potter type tailored jacket that it wore, the small arms outstretched in the mud. I imagined the child who had lost this toy, who had allowed it to fall from the window and was perhaps still asking plaintively what had happened to it.

Finally, I could stand it no more. I knew that I had to do something. I needed to rescue the rabbit from the side of the road. It was not easy to do this. The road at that point cuts through open countryside but it is narrow, and even at that time – twenty or more years ago – the traffic moved surprisingly fast. It wasn't easy to find a place to stop. I had to drive on more than four hundred yards until I could find a gateway where I could leave the car.

I walked back, stumbling along the uneven verge. It was four o'clock in the af-ternoon but the day was already darkening. The cars coming towards me cut through the rain with their headlights on. The drivers of those cars must have been wondering what I was doing walking along the verge. I was wondering that as well.

Eventually I drew close to the place where the toy must be. I could see it up ahead, those pathetic thin grey legs, the dull flash of the red jacket. But as I drew closer, I began to realize that my imagination had supplied many charming and pitiful details that were, in fact, entirely inaccurate.

The toy was not a rabbit, it was a little man, or something like a man. And the jacket was not a stylish Beatrix Potter coat but a red nylon fleece with peeling words printed on it in black. Coming level with the toy, I picked it up. Its face was stitched with an idiotic, toothy grin. A few more lines of stitching represented strands of hair. Sprouting from the top of its head was a piece of string and one of those rubber suckers that stick things to hard surfaces. The sucker had turned yellow and cracked. The fact that this figure wore a jumper but no trousers seemed faintly indecent. I reached down and picked it up. The worn words on the red jumper said: Big Hugs and Kisses.

So not a charming bunny but a goofy-looking little man with a retarded face and a sentimental slogan on his chest. What should I do? I was disappointed but I couldn't drop him back in the mud just because he wasn't what I expected him to be. So instead I turned and walked back with him dangling from my thumb and finger. I didn't want to touch him too much. He was wet and dirty. The rain blew into my face, muddy water from a passing car splashed across my boots.

I had not sent the donation I had meant to send to whatever cause we were meant to raise money for at that time... yet here I was rescuing lost toys from the verge

I felt stupid. I had not sent the donation I had meant to send to whatever cause we were meant to raise money for at that time – was it an earthquake in Japan, genocide in Rwanda? And neither had I informed myself sufficiently about whatever event we were meant to know about – the Oklahoma City bombing perhaps? Or was it The Balkans? Yet here I was rescuing lost toys from the verge – lost toys that weren't charming and loveable, but embarrassing and tacky.

Yet even in my mind, I couldn't insult the small person who I had found on the verge. That would have seemed cruel. When I finally got the children back from school, I took Big Hugs and Kisses out of the boot to show them. My twelve-year-old son was convulsed by laughter.

I know, I said. What was I doing? What was I doing?

You're bats, he said. Totally bats.

Yes – but I just couldn't leave him lying there.

My daughter, however, was only three and so was unconcerned by matters of taste. For her this was the acquisition of a new toy. She laughed at the conversation between me and my son but didn't really understand the joke. Instead she just wanted to play with Big Hugs and Kisses.

You'll have to put him in the washing machine, my son said.

Do you think we can?

You've got to try. He's all grubby. She can't play with him like that.

Yes, I think you're right. And maybe I should make him some trousers.What do you think? It doesn't seem quite right, does it? For him to have no trousers.

Mum, really, please, my son said.

Give me, give me, give me, my daughter wailed.

I told her that she would not be able to play with Big Hugs and Kisses until to-morrow, and put him in the washing machine. He survived the experience but didn't look much cleaner. His little grey legs were still stained at the knees and his face also continued to be marked by smudges of dirt. I put him on a radiator to dry and when my daughter came back from nursery the next day she was enchanted by him.

Big Hugs and Kisses, she said and gave him a big hug and a kiss.

—

After that Big Hugs and Kisses was always around the place. He would pop up occasionally in the bottom of a toy basket or stuffed down the back of the boot rack in the boiler room. Then, later, he appeared in the dust under my son's bunk bed. And after that, for several years, I think he was in a bag in the cupboard under the eaves, with other things I wanted to throw out but had not found time to take to the tip.

It's an interesting question, isn't it? What endures and what doesn't. I must have sorted through the toys quite often over the years. I would have sent some off to charity shops or passed them on to other children – but Big Hugs and Kisses survived every cull. Other toys we cared for more got broken or were accidentally left behind the sofas of holiday houses, yet somehow Big Hugs and Kisses always made it through.

We often joked about him over the years. My son took up my initial suggestion of trousers. You must make him some trousers, he would insist – but I never had time to follow up on this. My husband would hold Big Hugs and Kisses up by his cracked plastic sucker and tell friends the story of how I had rescued him from the side of the road, as an indication of how trivial I could be. My daughter, now old enough to under-stand that joke, would snatch him back and say that one mustn't judge by appearances. Big Hugs and Kisses, she would say, probably has a beautiful soul.

———

I'm not sure what this story is about. Is it about how love grows even when you don't think it will? Or does it simply demonstrate how a ridiculous inanimate object can sometimes ambush your emotions for no clear reason? Or perhaps it is just – as my daughter insists – about seeing beyond appearances.

I talk to my son about this on the day we find Big Hugs and Kisses in the dust under the bunk bed when we are sorting out his bedroom. My son is seventeen now and bored by me.

For God's sake, he says. Why do you have to be so weird? Not everything has a meaning. He's just a rather tasteless and dirty looking toy.

OK. I say. OK. You're quite right. Let's chuck him out.

I dangle him over the black bin bag.

No. No. You can't do that, my son says, snatching Big Hugs and Kisses back. For God's sake. He's part of the family.

Oh, is he? I thought he was just a rather tasteless toy.

Well, yes, he is – but still. You can't throw him out.

———

Then many years later, there comes a day when I realize – finally and conclusively – that my marriage is over, that my husband wishes to start a new life with another woman. I will have to leave the house that he and I have shared for more than thirty years. And there I am kneeling on the boiler room floor, sorting and sifting, keep this, keep that, chuck this, chuck that, trying, trying desperately to be positive.

And I open up a box of old toys that, earlier in the day, I pulled down from a high shelf. And as I open the box, I'm telling myself the story of what has happened to me. I am fifty-eight years old and my children have gone – gone happily, are having happy lives. And that's the thing no one tells you about being a successful parent, about creating children who can step out independently and successfully into the world. Yes, you have been a successful mother and it hurts like hell.

My hands sift through the box of toys. Among them is an appealing rabbit in a blue Beatrix Potter jacket. Only a year ago I had thought – oh good, we're through. We're safe, calmer waters now, so many struggles past. All those clichés of what you think old age will be. Then suddenly it is all gone and you try to be brave.

My hands run over a grey-brown moose and I remember the softness of his hair, his red felt nose. It really isn't a disaster, or only a small, polite disaster. I will be left with enough money to buy a little house or perhaps a flat. I'll do more work for the food bank, spend more time with friends. After all, over the years, there have been so many times when I wished them all gone. Before I was married, I travelled, worked, enjoyed the sense of swinging through the world with only the thin rope of my own abilities to keep me aloft.

A smiling teddy in a sun hat appears. He was my son's favourite for a while. Was his name Sonny? Or Billy? It isn't the same age fifty-eight. I am forced up tight against my own irrelevance. And despite that part of my mind that is brave and resolute, determined to lay aside bitterness and look to the future – yet still there is a dark panic that descends and will be difficult to lift.

It is Big Hugs and Kisses who I pull out from the bottom of the box. He grins up at me – that inane, relentless one-tooth grin – and I seize him and hold him close

In this moment it isn't the moose or the sun hat teddy I grasp. It is Big Hugs and Kisses who I pull out from the bottom of the box. He grins up at me – that inane, relentless one-tooth grin – and I seize him and hold him close. You can hardly see the letters now that say Big Hugs and Kisses. Why, why has he shared so much of our lives? Why am I so insanely strengthened just by holding him?

Mum, Mum, for God's sake. Why are you so weird? Not everything has a meaning. But still I want to know, I want to be able to tell a story, a better story than my own story, a story that has a proper end. A story that says – this is what you should understand about this. Big Hugs and Kisses and I continue to sit on the boiler room floor, stubbornly lacking in proper story. Perhaps what matters is simply that Big Hugs and Kisses exists. He is still here. I am still here. He and I both know these facts. I look down again at his one tooth smile, the brightness that somehow fills his eyes, although they are only lines of stitching. Big Hugs and Kisses has an instinct for survival and a talent for enjoying his life. I must make him some trousers, I really must. **H**

COMING SOON.
8 CHAPBOOKS.
8 DUTCH WRITERS.
8 TRANSLATIONS.

VERZET is a collection of beautifully designed chapbooks, showcasing the work of eight of the most exciting young writers working in the Netherlands today superbly rendered into English by a new generation of translators.

The list includes an impressive array of award winners and nominees who are long overdue their English language translations.

**PUBLISHED BY STRANGERS PRESS:
22ND SEPTEMBER 2020**

AVAILABLE FROM GOOD BOOKSHOPS
AND FROM WWW.STRANGERS.PRESS/SHOP

nieuw new
dutch **nederlands**
stemmen voices

New Dutch Writing is a campaign from the Dutch Foundation for
Literature and Modern Culture to promote Dutch writing in translation in
the UK. For more information please go to www.newdutchwriting.co.uk

ON THE BEACH

by *Alexander Williamson*

On the beach he found a damaged golf ball among a crop of stones. The plastic coating had weathered away, disclosing the yellow core underneath. It resembled a perfectly poached egg, the flaccid white encasing a silky yolk, or the cross-sectional diagram of a planet from a child's science book. He held it and considered it for a while, then dropped it onto his foot and kicked it over the sand. Many years before he had played golf on a beach like this, in the company of his uncle and younger cousin, at Abersoch in north Wales. He would have been ten or eleven years old. Golf loomed large in his life back then, although technically they weren't actually playing golf but hitting balls up and down the empty beach and watching the wind play havoc with their shots.

At the time, his uncle had a dog that liked to chew golf balls. A soft golden Labrador named Tizer. In homage, or so he believed, to the fizzy drink from Cumbernauld, which was the colour of dehydrated urine. Tizer wasn't remotely Tizer-coloured, but his coat bore just enough of a resemblance for the name to have taken root in his uncle's mind. Or perhaps it was just that his uncle really liked the drink. In his grandparents' chalet at Abersoch he saw Tizer destroy an old golf ball in a matter of seconds, peeling back the dimpled plastic and crushing the compressed bundle of rubber string that made up its inner core, the part which gave the ball weight and flight. After which Tizer slumped his head down onto his outstretched paws, his muzzle mussed with slobber and white plastic shards, and emitted a long, guttural groan. He couldn't remember Tizer being on the beach while they hit golf balls that damp day in July, but he was bound to have been out there somewhere, sniffing the salt air and scampering among the dunes, tail whipping the air like a propeller.

———

In *The Gay Science*, Nietzsche declared: *I have given a name to my pain and call it 'dog': it is just as faithful, just as importunate and shameless, just as entertaining, just as wise, as any other dog, and I can domineer over it, and vent my bad humour over it.*

Nietzsche, famously, suffered with ill health all his life. Headaches in childhood, an accident while vaulting a horse during his military training, constant trouble with his bowels and stomach, bouts of vomiting, encroaching blindness and eventual dementia, the latter caused not, as was once assumed, by syphilis during a youthful visit to a brothel, but by a slowly developing brain tumour, a similar condition to that which brought about his father Carl Ludwig's untimely death at the age of thirty-five. The diagnosis: *softening of the brain.*

Nietzsche's perpetual ill health made his list of injuries look like nothing more than the bumps and scrapes of childhood. Which, of course, they were

In fact, Nietzsche's perpetual ill health made his list of injuries look like nothing more than the bumps and scrapes of childhood. Which, of course, they were. And yet, when Nietzsche wrote of his pain, he felt that the philosopher wasn't simply referring to this litany of physical ailments, but the pain of self-overcoming [*Selbstüberwindung*] and the pain of his Godlessness, both of which became the basis of his faith in himself, his philosophy and his writing, an antithetical process no less fraught with discomfort. In later life, Nietzsche's bad faith became a war on two fronts, bringing him into conflict with those he loved and held dear, such as Richard and Cosima Wagner, and driving him into hallucinatory derangement and near-penury, until he became reliant on the financial support of his mother, Franziska, and the less-than-benevolent advances of his sociopathic younger sister, Elisabeth.

When he was young, all was hope and dream and possibility, the possibility that one day something truly wonderful would happen. The aphorisms and proverbs of the Bible and prescriptions of Erasmus' *Adagia*, which he first became aware of in childhood, taught him that through diligence, endeavour and good faith, he would realise his dreams.

If at first you don't succeed. Get up and dust yourself down. Mighty oaks from tiny acorns grow. Don't count all your chickens. Never look a gift horse in the mouth. Good things come to those who wait. That which doesn't kill you, makes you stronger.

He waited. Nothing happened.

He read the Delphic maxims, ancient Grecian codes for a certain mode of morality which ranged from the gnomic to the instructive. *Follow God. Respect the law. Respect your parents. Be overcome by justice. Know what you have learned. Perceive what you have heard. Think as a mortal. Control yourself. Love friends. Honor the house.*

Over time, the simplicity of those proverbs and prescriptions became complicated or tempered by other, more ambivalent mantras, which now moved to the forefront of his consciousness. *Children should be seen and not heard. Do not speak unless spoken to. Ignorance is bliss. Nothing will come of nothing. Don't let the bastards grind you down. Failure is not an option. The way up and the way down are the same. The road of excess leads to the palace of wisdom. Try again. Fail again. Fail better.*

[Nietzsche: *Become what you are.*]

—

Much later, too late to prosper from it, he
encountered the Aristotelian concept of *eudaimonia*
and *ēthikē aretē*, the pursuit of happiness and self-
becoming through the wellness of spirit and
virtuousness, and its alternate others, anhedonia,
the reluctance and inability to experience pleasure,
and hedonophobia, the persistent fear of pleasure.

He thought of his mother, her unhappiness before
and after her illness. How he had failed her.

—

[*Because you are always miserable.*]

—

He found it interesting that Nietzsche associated
self-knowledge with pain. For he often felt the
keenness of the observation. Becoming what he
was had been painful. Knowing himself more so.
Walking, too, was uncomfortable, but not the pain
of walking – sore feet, blisters, aching limbs and the
like – but the notion that he was always walking
away from his past rather than towards his future;
as though his life were something he could escape,
and that one day he would. Even though, according

to Nietzsche, that would mean living his life all over again.

Nietzsche: *This life as you now live it and have lived it you will have to live again; and there will be nothing new in it, but every pain and every joy and every thought and sigh and everything unspeakably small or great in your life must return to you, all in the same success and sequence... The eternal hourglass of existence is turned over and over again, and you with it, speck of dust!*

The grain of sand through which you encounter the world. Like Narcissus contemplating his reflection. Like writing a memoir at the age of forty

A speck of dust. The grain of sand through which you encounter the world. Like Narcissus contemplating his reflection. Like writing a memoir at the age of forty.

Forty. A laughable milestone. Joyce's age when he published *Ulysses*. Beckett's when he penned *First Love*. Kierkegaard when he published *Fear and Trembling*. Orwell when he began *Animal Farm*. Henry Miller – *Tropic of Cancer*. Hemingway when he wrote *For Whom the Bell Tolls*. Bukowski when his first book of poems came out. Herzog when he made *Fitzcarraldo*. Lennon when Chapman shot him dead. BS Johnson when he slit his wrists.

His father's childhood friend, who dropped dead in the shower from a heart attack following his morning swim at Abersoch.

Forty. *The old age of youth*, according to Victor Hugo. The moment when time accelerates, just as one's ability to comprehend it slows. The hinge-point. The turning. The end of the beginning. The beginning of the end.

At sixteen, he could not picture his fortieth birthday. By his thirties, he realised he was creeping into the frame. He had vaguely hoped it would be at the centre of some Dionysian carnival in the Balearics or the Cyclades, surrounded by the huge circle of friends he had amassed over the years, some of whom had flown in to surprise him. A far cry from the prosaic reality of the day when it finally arrived.

Forty. *The old age of youth*, according to Victor Hugo. The moment when time accelerates, just as one's ability to comprehend it slows

Impossible to imagine how he would rise in the morning, perhaps after making love to his wife, sleepily embrace the small, warm bodies of his children, before descending into the kitchen, sitting down to open the cards and gifts from a handful of friends and family, and feeling wounded by their generosity, their kindness, despite the great distances between them. Then, as was customary, his wife would go to work, and he would take his children to school in a muggy veil of drizzle, returning home to shower and shave, and to contemplate his face in the mirror; the unremarkable face written in his hybrid genes, his mother's eyes and his father's jawline, the face he deserved, ten years in advance of Orwell's deadline, which did not please him, which whenever he caught sight of it he had to turn away.

The self his body presented to the world. His face, like his mother's, was crinkled with crow's feet, and his forehead lined and creased. His hairline, slowly receding since his late teens, was now on the point of disappearing altogether, much like his father's. Their resemblance, frequently remarked upon by friends and family, had become inevitable. His body was carrying him into old age, where it would leave him, and he would leave it. The imprint of the years upon it and the hint of worse to come. He could feel it approaching, like a train slowing as it enters a station.

—

[*I have given a name to my pain and call it Memory.*]

—

He read about an experiment conducted by an American psychologist in the late 1960s. Three groups of dogs were placed in yoked harnesses. The first group of dogs were kept in the harness for a short while before being released. The second group of dogs were given a series of electric shocks at random, which they could stop by pressing a lever. The third pair of dogs were shocked repeatedly, but unlike the second pair of dogs, they were not given a lever to stop the shocks. After being shocked repeatedly without respite, the third group of dogs came to understand that their suffering was inescapable, and in subsequent experiments, simply submitted to it. The scientist labelled the condition *learned helplessness*.

—

[Strindberg: *I loathe people who keep dogs. They are cowards who haven't got the guts to bite people themselves.*]

—

The apparent social intelligence of dogs has prompted a number of scientific investigations into the canine psyche, resulting in a raft of popular science books with titles such as *A Dog's Purpose*, *The Genius of Dogs*, *How Dogs Love Us*, *At the Other End of the Leash*. After his golden Labrador died, John Grogan, then a journalist, memorialised his beloved pet in a bestselling autobiography, *Marley and Me*, which was later made into a Hollywood movie, a tearjerker starring Owen Wilson and Jennifer Aniston, the success of which spawned a series of children's books further essaying Marley's hapless antics, following in the footprints of Spot, Shiloh, Old Yeller, What-a-mess, Kipper, Hairy Maclary and countless others. He couldn't blame Grogan. Sometimes it paid to keep it simple. Perhaps he should write about dogs. Take photographs of dogs. Or paint them.

Aesthetic representations of dogs were traceable to prehistoric times. Grogan's cave-dwelling ancestors first sketched dog-like figures onto the walls of dank caves, while Grecian and Roman potters studded their ceramics with canine imagery, and Cerberus stalked through the Underworld. As a dog's purpose changed from hunter's retriever to companionable pet, so their presence in paintings, particularly portraits, proliferated. The Magnum photographer Elliott Erwitt's street-snapped portraits of dogs and their owners catalogued the evolution of canine companionship in the contemporary mode, while William Wegman's colour portraits of Weimaraners were to Flemish Primitivism what the book *Marley and Me* and its cinematic adaptation were to High Modernism and the Golden Age of Hollywood. C.M. Coolidge's anthropomorphised dogs playing cards, which borrowed scenes from Caravaggio and Paul Cezanne, played with aesthetic tradition in a more sophisticated way than Wegman's hang-dog subjects.

Books about dogs and films about dogs and paintings of dogs and photographs of dogs and sculptures of dogs

Books about dogs and films about dogs and paintings of dogs and photographs of dogs and sculptures of dogs and, less frequently, TV programmes about dogs. *The Adventures of Rin Tin Tin. Lassie. Benji. Scooby-Doo. Droopy. Huckleberry Hound. Woof! Paw Patrol* – a favourite of his children. Not to mention the shows where dogs were a key part of the ensemble. Sweep in *Sooty and Co.* Johnny Briggs and his dog Razzle. Watching episodes of *The Littlest Hobo* as a child had taught him about solitude and sorrow; the little dog who solves a problem, and then moves on to the next town. Never settles, never stays. *Until tomorrow, I'll just keep moving on.* Even today, the first bars of the theme tune triggered a wave of sadness he could not endure.

———

A dog's purpose. What was it about dogs that so preoccupied him? Their obedience? Their servility? Their desire to be loved by people who anthropomorphised them, treated them like children or beat them without mercy? There was something about the human-canine relationship that made his flesh crawl. How his mother had spoken to their dog when it was having a phantom pregnancy, fussing over its toys in its basket. Yet for all their apparent domestication, dogs were scavengers who, given half the chance, would ransack a kitchen, annihilate prized possessions, and drop a crap on a pedestrian-heavy road. Then there were those deviant breeds who were sired for the specific purpose of mauling to death vulnerable family members left in their watchful care. As an infant he was bitten by his parents' dog, a large, bad-tempered, male black Labrador who didn't like his ears being pulled, particularly not by small, usurping children. He was lucky. A different breed and he may not have lived to tell the tale. And yet he understood the nature of the relationship, the purpose of canine companionship, how it could lift a person from the deepest depression, brighten the bleakest day. And there was the rub, the departure of a beloved four-legged friend from an emotionally dependent owner was almost always traumatic, presaged either by the solemnity of drawn-out disintegration or the indignity of finding itself unable to lift itself from a puddle of its own shit. Dogs and humans shared an inescapable fate.

—

Walking on the beach he thought of another dog, the enigmatic canine in the foreground on the cover of the Canadian singer-songwriter Neil Young's second album: *Everybody Knows This Is Nowhere*. He was unsure of the breed of the dog, but by process of elimination narrowed it down to an American White Shepherd. Young had apparently named the animal Winnipeg after the city in Manitoba where he and his mother relocated after his parents separated. The dog featured in several photographs of Young from the late sixties and early seventies, mostly taken by Henry Diltz at Young's Broken Arrow Ranch in California.

The grain of the film used for the portrait ... gives the album cover the appearance of a pointillist painting; raw and unpolished like the music inside

The grain of the film used for the portrait of Young gives the album cover the appearance of a pointillist painting; raw and unpolished like the music inside. A man without possessions, other than his dog. Ironically, it recalls Thomas

Gainsborough's portraits of *Colonel John Bullock* and *An officer of the 4th Regiment of Foot*. Young leaning against a tree, his faithful dog at his side, the peaks and valleys of Topanga Canyon, then home for Young, in the background.

Searching the internet, he came across other photographs of Young with dogs which served to underscore his lonesome hippy-boy persona. Here were career-spanning photographs of Young hugger-mugger with some hound or other. This even extended to the stuffed dog in the foreground of a band portrait of Crosby, Stills, Nash & Young, which appeared on the cover of their 1970 album *Déjà-Vu*. Like that of his earlier solo album, this portrait reflects Young's enduring fascination with Americana and frontier mythology, which his next solo album, *After the Gold Rush*, would develop further.

He came across [Neil] Young's rangy, scrawny music by accident, when flicking through his parents' CD collection, a selection as uninspired as it was sparse

The most recent photo he had seen was taken from the rear of Young's *Hitchhiker* album. The photo is dated 1976 and shows Young walking up a beach, sun just about to dip under the horizon, his narrow frame slim as his shadow. A few strides ahead of him, yet another nameless dog lopes in the surf.

He came across Young's rangy, scrawny music by accident, when flicking through his parents' CD collection, a selection as uninspired as it was sparse. Among the Paul Simon, Tears for Fears and Steely Dan albums there was Young's *Harvest* of 1972 – his best-selling, most enduring and, some might say, most endearing album. The Neil Young album most people had heard of. Later he learned that his father was a fan of Crosby, Stills, Nash & Young, though without any actual commitment to having acquired the ensemble's records. Tellingly, his parents also owned a copy of America's *Greatest Hits*, the band whose sound was so indebted to Harvest-era Young that they sounded like a tribute act; and who knocked Young's 'Heart of Gold' off the top of the singles chart with their derivative imitation, 'Horse With No Name'.

—

For a time, he had become obsessed with Neil Young. His music, his looks, his life. His refusal to compromise. As a young man, he had seen in Young's process of self-overcoming a route map to guide his own, a snaking path from the mundane present into an unknown future. A self-professed loner, Young possessed a determination, a will-to-power that was positively Nietzschean, but it was a will-to-power entirely lacking in himself. When the time came for him to make his move, he froze. Talked himself out of it. Buried himself in the sand.

—

On the Beach drew from the deep well of emotional privations and psychic turmoil that coloured the early Seventies; a decadent, self-centred decade when the collective aspirations of the flower children had been swept away by a landslide of political disturbance which bordered on the anarchic. The messy end to the Vietnam War. Watergate rumbling on. Los Angeles spooked by murders committed under the orders of self-styled guru and commune leader Charles Manson, whom Young had known from his Topanga Canyon days, later reflecting with typical understatement that the songwriter-turned-cult leader *didn't handle rejection well*. Young's relationship with the actress Carrie Snodgress was by now in terminal decline. Their son, Zeke, had been diagnosed with cerebral palsy shortly after his birth. Then there was the loss of Danny Whitten, Crazy Horse's guitarist and Young's soul brother, who had overdosed on the eve of the Harvest tour after Young fired him from the band.

Save for its opener, 'Walk On', the songs of *On the Beach* are weighed down by sorrow and loss. Young's lyrics, frequently spare, are simplistic to the point of banality, yet unflinchingly spare and direct. Specific events and interpersonal issues are unpicked and rewoven: the disastrous *Harvest* tour, the implosion of CSNY, the Manson murders, his relationship with Carrie, Nixon's duplicitousness. Ecological disaster. Violent revolution. A coming apocalypse.

There was something more abject in the grizzled persona of this Young than that at the decade's inception: the lonely boy out on the weekend. Young's music, which up to that point had been elegiac in its marriage of American mythology with the counter-cultural considerations, was now more circumspect, more entropic. *On the Beach* had a retrospective quality, a critically self-assessing eye, a composite portrait of the creative individual's place in the world.

Los Angeles spooked by murders committed under the orders of self-styled guru and commune leader Charles Manson, whom Young had known

Young was twenty-eight years old when he made *On the Beach*, a culmination of three records of such bleakness many critics at the time worried about his state of mind. Now it was widely considered to be the high-water mark of his career. Success for Young came early, fast and hard. He'd first tasted it with Buffalo Springfield when he was barely twenty-one. Small wonder that he felt washed up. But Young was lucky. He'd come out the other side, largely unscathed. Others from that time weren't so fortunate.

Despite the album's prevailing mood of subdued bleakness, at certain moments *On the Beach* hymned a quietly restorative beauty, most evident in the consoling strains of the interweaving harmonica and fiddle on 'Ambulance Blues'. The song, much like 'Don't Be Denied', offered another journey through the past, one spiritually redeeming and restorative for the musician.

On the album cover, the desaturated, honeyed yellows of the surrealistic totems assembled on a beach — a parasol, two folding chairs, Young clad in jacket and slacks, the fin of a buried Cadillac — were counter-posed with the bleached out sand and sky, the grey sliver of water. His back to the camera,

Young faced the ocean, the worries of the world and the vicissitudes of success behind him. He was watching the water, looking out on a vast emptiness, with one eye turned inward, connecting nothing with nothing, and recording everything.

I was pretty down I guess at the time, but I just did what I wanted to do, at that time. I think if everybody looks back at their own lives they'll realise that they went through something like that. There's periods of depression, periods of elation, optimism and scepticism, the whole thing is… it just keeps coming in waves.

He was watching the water, looking out on a vast emptiness, with one eye turned inward, connecting nothing with nothing, and recording everything

You go down to the beach and watch the same thing, just imagine every wave is a different set of emotions coming in. Just keep coming. As long as you don't ignore it, it'll still be there. If you start shutting yourself off and not letting yourself live through the things that are coming through you, I think that's when people start getting old really fast, that's when they really age. 'Cause they decide that, they're happy to be what they were at a certain time in their lives when they were the happiest, and they say 'that's where I'm gonna be for the rest of my life'. From that minute on they're dead, y'know, just walking around.

———

[Where are you going with this?]

———

Some years after the death of their first black Labrador, his parents acquired another. Home from university, he had gone with his mother to collect the puppy from a farm a short distance away. When they arrived, the breeder led them to a small shed in the yard. A welter of small cries emanated from inside, and when she opened the shed it was full of Labrador puppies tumbling over one another. The breeder handed one to his mother, and she passed it to him. As he cradled the puppy in his arms he thought, *This must be how it feels to become a father.*

They named the dog Peg, after the Steely Dan song.

After university, when he was back living with his parents, directionless, rootless and restless, Peg became his closest companion. In the morning he would wake to the sound of her paws scratching the floorboards on the landing, followed by sniffing and whining at the gap under the door. In those days of doing nothing while figuring out what his something should be, they took long walks through the Cheshire fields, him stoned or ruminating anxiously, Peg springing along the path up ahead. Come the evening, she would sit with him as he read or listened to music in his room. After he left home, his mother reported how the dog would disappear in the evening, how she often found the dog lying on his bed.

Peg became a different kind of dog after he left, mollycoddled and neurotic, spoilt with scraps from the table, welcomed on the furniture. His mother, frequently depressive and antisocial, used the dog as a reason to avoid human contact, addressing her as one would an infant in the presence of their friends. After his mother's illness, the dog's health also began to suffer. She became increasingly prone to tremors and fits. His parents, fearful of the passing of their beloved pet, allowed her condition to worsen. He visited frequently that year and often felt that her decline mirrored that of his mother. His mother was now short-tempered with the dog, as irritable as she was with everyone else. The nadir came when, one evening over dinner, the aged dog began to defecate in the kitchen and his mother walked behind her with a sheet of kitchen roll pressed against her anus. Not long after that the dog refused to leave her bed and his parents took her on that final, long-dreaded but inevitable visit to the vet.

With his father he'd taken Peg to the beach once, on another wide expanse of sand just outside Rhyl. They had talked of going to Abersoch but didn't make it that far. He remembers little of their conversation. Possibly they talked about his aspirations, his plans for the future. Perhaps they didn't speak at all. He remembered that the dog, off her lead, ran to a family eating their lunch and scared their little girl. *Keep her on the lead, please mate*, the man said. *Sorry*, said his father, slipping her back onto the leash. On the beach that day, he had taken some photographs with the old Canon camera his father had given him. Once upon a time photography had interested his father, before life and work took over. Some weeks prior he had discovered a folder containing black and white prints his father had developed twenty years earlier.

Portraits of his parents and their friends from before he was born, several of him as a newborn and a pack of black Labrador puppies, looking plaintively at the camera.

——

An early memory. Aged four or five. Playing with the boy from next door in his parents' back garden. Jimmy. Jimmy is almost a year older than him, with straw-coloured hair, a stocky physique and piggy eyes. An elder sibling, with a younger sister. Usually they talk to each other through the privet hedge at the bottom of the garden, but today Jimmy has been allowed to come over to play. Left to their own devices he and the boy from next door have discovered a new and dangerous game. Out of sight of the kitchen window, where his mother is feeding his younger brother, they take it in turns to call his parents' black Labrador to them, distracting the dog so the other can hit it across the hind legs with a stick. Emitting a low growl, the dog turns in uncertain circles, before chasing them across the garden, where they take refuge in the low branches of the small apple tree. Being older, Jimmy is faster, stronger, and more adept at climbing the tree. Jimmy's family do not own a dog, or any other pets. He does not have many other friends. Hitting the dog was his idea.

——

[I have given a name to my dog and call it Learned Helplessness.] **H**

RSL Awards & Prizes
now open for submissions

RSL Literature Matters Awards 2021

These Awards provide financial support to undertake a **new piece of writing or literary project**. Priority will be given to proposals which help connect with audiences/topics outside the usual reach of literature, and/or help generate public discussion about why literature matters.

Projects could include a piece or pieces of writing, a publication, an event, a production, on any subject and in any form, including (but not limited to) prose fiction or non-fiction, short stories, poetry, playwriting, screenwriting, graphic fiction, biography or travel-writing. The Awards are open to UK residents and there is there is a total of £20,000 available to be distributed across a number of projects.

RSL Christopher Bland Prize 2021

The **£10,000** RSL Christopher Bland Prize aims to encourage and celebrate older writers and is awarded annually to a debut novelist or popular non-fiction writer, **first published at the age of 50 or over** in the calendar year 2020. The 2021 Prize is open for publishers or agents to submit works by authors writing in English from the United Kingdom and the Republic of Ireland.

Visit rsliterature.org for full details.

JOIN US!

Membership makes the perfect gift!

RSL Membership
and
RSL Young Person's Membership
(for under 30s)

£60/£40 a year for first year,
reducing to £50/30 a year thereafter

- Attend all of our **events** free of charge
- Subscribe free to our magazine *RSL Review*
- Attend our online **Book Clubs** free of charge
- Take advantage of **exclusive offers** with our partner organisations
- Free **RSL 200 Virginia Woolf tote bag** for all new Members
- Support our **charitable aims** as the national voice for the value of literature

RSL Gift Membership

👉 **Thinking ahead to the festive season?
Scan to find out more about
RSL Gift Membership.**

rsliterature.org

Nearly City

by Ashley Hickson-Lovence

Two years ago I left Hackney for Norwich and, on a whim, purchased a Canaries – Norwich City Football Club's nickname – home shirt in the end-of-season sale; I now consider myself a fan of sorts. A few months back, predictably aware of my new-found fandom, YouTube recommended I watch: 'When Norwich Nearly Won the Premier League.' Having just witnessed a season where Norwich resoundingly finished bottom of the league, the story of their near-title triumph seemed unthinkable. As the video played, my eyes were drawn to one figure in particular: Ruel Fox, who played an integral part in City's audacious crusade to clinch their first ever Premier League title.

English football changed forever in 1992. After years of chronic financial mismanagement, dilapidated stadiums and rising hooliganism, the Premier League was formed to replace Football League's First Division as the new top league in the country. During its inaugural season, and among the giants of the game – Manchester United, Liverpool and Arsenal – it was little Norwich City who nearly won it, with the help of fan-favourite Ruel Fox on the wing.

Fox's rise to one of the Premier League's best began in 1968. Of Montserratian descent, Fox was born and raised in Ipswich (Norwich's arch-rivals), and grew up on a housing estate with his mum on the outskirts of town. It was while playing for local semi-professional side Whitton United as a teenager that professional clubs came calling. Following an unsuccessful trial at Ipswich Town first, Fox made his way up the A140 to train with the Canaries, and within two days was snapped up.

The mid-eighties weren't an easy time to be a Black footballer anywhere in the UK but especially not in rural Norfolk, even with the likes of fellow players Louie Donawa and Dale Gordon already at the club. Just five years before Fox joined, Justin Fashanu, Britain's first openly gay footballer, had also made a name at Norwich before moving onto Brian Clough's Nottingham Forest.

Like any teenager flying the nest for the first time, Fox didn't find the move to the city easy initially. Norwich is only forty miles from Ipswich, but for a young Fox living in digs in the centre of the city, it felt like a million. In an interview with the *Eastern Daily Press* in 2016[1], Fox admitted that it wasn't until he arrived at Norwich that he experienced racism first-hand. Some of the abuse came from his own teammates: 'I can't lie … the first time I encountered racism to any great extent was when I started playing for Norwich, and some of it came from lads in my team'. Fox added that he was subject to 'a lot of little snidey things like, "Pick up the blackie" and that sort of thing'.

Despite this environment of racial abuse, Fox shone on the pitch, making his debut for the Canaries at the age of 17 in a League Cup match against Coventry City — and soon established himself as a valued member of the first-team squad. Fox emerged as an old-school four-four-two winger, bamboozling full-backs (including future England-regulars Stuart Pearce and Graeme Le Saux), shifting one way, then the other, breezing to the byline and drilling it into the box for the striker – usually teammates Robert Fleck or Chris Sutton – to head home.

Despite this promising start to life as a Canary, Fox's time at Carrow Road wasn't always straightforward. On top of the racism he endured, he failed to hold down a permanent place in the first eleven and, frustrated by his lack of minutes leading up to the start of the 1992/1993 season, was close to leaving the club. The favourites to acquire

---

1 https://www.edp24.co.uk/sport/norwich-city/ruel-fox-i-first-encountered-racism-at-norwich-city-even-in-our-dressing-room-1-4728691

his signature: Dutch giants Ajax. But, following the sale of Dale Gordon to Rangers, new manager Mike Walker, recently promoted from his role as youth team manager, persuaded Fox to stay.

By the start of Norwich City's first campaign in the newly formed 'Premier League', the club were odds-on favourites to go down, having finished a lowly 18th the previous season. Star striker Robert Fleck left for Chelsea for a record fee of £2.1 million, so it fell upon the shoulders of Chris Sutton, new signing Mark Robins and, of course, Ruel Fox to step up to the plate and provide the goals Norwich needed to compete.

Despite efforts of club legend Bryan Gunn in goal, Blackburn Rovers battered them 7-1 at Ewood Park, with striker Alan Shearer helping himself to a brace

Surprising many, City made a blistering start to the season, after falling behind 2-0 in their opening game to title-favourites Arsenal, Norwich turned the tie around in the second half to win 4-2, with Fox himself scoring an 84th minute goal. Four days later, they went on to beat Chelsea.

But by October, cracks were beginning to appear and the Canaries of the previous season threatened to resurface. Despite efforts of club legend Bryan Gunn in goal, Blackburn Rovers battered them 7-1 at Ewood Park, with striker Alan Shearer helping himself to a brace. Three weeks later, the team suffered a 4-1 defeat to Liverpool.

Norwich hit their stride again with wins against Oldham Athletic and Aston Villa, and by

Christmas, found themselves back in title contention, sitting eight points clear at the top of the league.

Pressure on the minnows began to build in the new year, and three defeats in April, including a demoralising 3-0 loss to rivals Ipswich Town — put paid to any early title hopes. After thirty-eight games, the unlikely dream was over: Norwich finished third, two points behind Aston Villa in second, and twelve points behind Manchester United. Close but not close enough.

Norwich hit their stride again... and by Christmas, found themselves back in title contention, sitting eight points clear at the top of the league

Fox started thirty-four times and scored four goals in this, Norwich City's record-breaking campaign. And, by finishing third – their highest-ever league finish – the Canaries did qualify for the UEFA Cup for the first time, a development that would allow them to play – and go on to beat – the mighty Bayern Munich on their own patch the following season. Of course, Fox played an integral part in that historic night too, but that's a story for another day. ◫

Overexposed

by Nick Bradley

oday, I'd like to unearth a time in my life when I wasn't very happy. To pick the scabs off a period when I didn't feel creative at all. When I spent two hours a day on crowded trains, commuting from where I lived on one side of Tokyo city to the other, where I worked.

I would ride the train and — in between berating myself for having achieved nothing by the age of thirty — listen to gloomy albums on my iPod, compose awful poetry on my smartphone, read novels endlessly on my Kindle, and plan my escape from the city.

About once a month, I'd be sent to far-flung parts of the country by my company to somewhere picturesque, where I would be guided around by people like Hori-san on Sado Island, who during his twenties had fled Tokyo for a better life on the island where he was raised. I would eat delicious food, stay in five-star hotels and traditional Japanese inns, bathe in onsen, and take glossy photographs of all of these things for the websites my company produced. From a distance, my life probably looked great.

But then I would return to my pitiful life in the city. After spending time with my guide on Sado Island, Hori-san's words echoed in my ears:

'People in Tokyo… their faces are dying.'

Looking at some of my photos here, you might see what he means.

Back in the office I'd either write the text that accompanied the glossy travel photos, or I'd be given a text in Japanese to translate into English.

Once again, commuting to and from the office.

However, one thing I also did on my commute each day was to carry a small compact Fujifilm 35mm camera, which used a special film (now obsolete) called Natura Classica. This film was 1600 ISO, which meant it was extremely sensitive, and good in low light conditions without a flash. I slipped this small, beautiful camera into a pocket on my satchel, and I carried it to and from the office every day, pulling it out surreptitiously now and again to capture anything on my commute which caught my eye.

The images in this photo essay are picked from the four or five rolls of film I shot during those commutes, not from the tens of thousands of glossy, digital photos I shot for my job

Looking at them now, I'm struck by their gritty bleakness. They are grainy, blurred and somewhat depressing. A lot of them are, technically, very bad photos. But they somehow contain more 'flavour' (as they say in Japanese) than the professional photos I was taking with my DSLR from the same era.

They remind me of the gloominess and pain, that strange breed of darkness and creativity that I found myself drawing upon, from deep within myself, when I wrote my first novel *The Cat and The City*.

I say 'my first novel', but what I mean is 'the first novel I wrote that was published'.

Because now, looking at the photos I've chosen to accompany this piece, I'm starting to think about the photos that didn't make the cut, just like those hundreds of thousands of words I wrote before *The Cat and The City*. All those words I kept to myself, and never showed anyone, or tried to get published.

—

When I look up the word 'hinterland' in the *Oxford English Dictionary*, I'm struck particularly by the second definition:

> *An area lying beyond what is visible or known: the strange hinterland where life begins and ends.*

And then I'm also struck by the etymology of the word:

> *ORIGIN*
> *late 19th century: from German,*
> *from hinter 'behind' + Land 'land'.*

The phrase 'beyond what is visible or known' has got me thinking about concepts of creativity – composition, in the sense of both a photograph, but also in the sense of writing – specifically, what we cut out, what we leave out when we present work to people. What has always drawn me to photography is not necessarily what Henri Cartier-Bresson defined as 'the decisive moment'. What makes a photo interesting to me is the portrayal within the frame of what lies outside it. When composing a photograph, an essay, or a short story, sometimes what we leave out is just as interesting as what we present to a viewer or reader. The negative space in a photograph can sometimes speak just as powerfully as the subject of the photograph.

> **When composing a photograph, an essay, or a short story, sometimes what we leave out is just as interesting as what we present to a viewer or reader**

And the photos themselves. What do they tell us about the photographer?

What is this person not telling me?

What is going on outside the frame?

What is going on inside the photographer? (And does this even matter?)

When I look at these photos, what do they tell me about the person I was back then? Can I still see the depression I felt at the time within the frame? Can I still feel the desperation that I felt on my lunch breaks, that desire to write novels and short stories? Is it visible in these photos, outside the frame? And what is this creeping sense of nostalgia I feel tugging at my stomach when I look over these images? How is it I can feel nostalgic for a time in which I sometimes thought about ending my own life?

Or am I nostalgic for the film itself? The very film on which the photos are captured? The film that has now been discontinued, that cannot be purchased anymore.

Do I miss this quiet period of uninterrupted photographic creativity I experienced in Tokyo?

—

I remember the joy of taking photos on film. Of spreading the roll out over what could be a month, or several months. Waiting for those moments that could perhaps be captured. Wondering whether that shot you thought was perfect at the time would come out OK. Waiting to get them processed. The disappointment at seeing how badly the shot you thought would be incredible came out; the surprise at something that you didn't even consider at the time revealing itself like a poem.

DSLRs replaced film cameras.
Mirrorless cameras replaced DSLRs.
Now they've all been replaced by smartphones.

My DSLR rests snugly inside its case. I've barely taken any photos on it in the past couple of years. I've been writing more, photographing less. But I still look at my old photographs when I write. These photos ceased to be things I showed to other people, and became things I kept for myself. Fragments of a life I'd lived and lost.

Something I could never get back again. ▉

All the world's writing, all the year round.

Since 1984, *Wasafiri* has championed global voices, bringing together the best creative and critical writing from the world's leading authors.

Wasafiri 104, on post-conflict literature, featuring Juan Gabriel Vásquez, Yolande Mukagasana, and Juliane Okot Bitek, is out now.

You thought you knew the whole story...

Come and celebrate with us at Untitled writers' events - a new platform for underrepresented writers to share their work in front of an audience. There are no limitations to what might be shared and we know there'll be something for everyone.

To find out more about Untitled, let us know if you want to share your work in the future and to find news about our next event in October visit **untitledwriting.co.uk**

🐦 writinguntitled   📷 untitled_writing

IN CONVERSATION WITH

Helen Smith

Historian and writer Susan Karen Burton interviewed Helen Smith, author of The Uncommon Reader: A Life of Edward Garnett, *a Sunday Times book of the year. They discussed the role of the editor, the increasing popularity of non-fiction and the advantages and disadvantages of writing about the dead.*

Susan Karen Burton: *The Uncommon Reader* is a biography of 'mentor and editor of literary genius,' Edward Garnett. Who was he?

Helen Smith: Edward Garnett was a remarkable man. I think the thing that I found most extraordinary about him was his sheer capacity for reading and commenting on manuscripts, most of which were not very good and were going to be rejected. He came from quite a literary background. His father was Keeper of Printed Books at the British Museum, and Garnett fell into the role of publisher's reader. He didn't go to university. He got a very menial job packing up books for posting out at T. Fisher Unwin and he just progressed from there. He very quickly got out of the packing department and started reading manuscripts and that was it, that was his life's calling.

SKB: You say most of the manuscripts were going to be rejected. So because of him they were published? What did he do to these manuscripts to turn them into publishable works?

HS: Garnett's great talent was to spot latent talent in other writers. He had an unerring eye. One of his enduring battles throughout his career was with this idea that publishers couldn't recognise really good writing. There was this tension between the commercial imperative and the advancement of truly great literary writing. 'They don't know' was his great lament, that publishers couldn't see good writers or they rejected good writers on a commercial basis. That's not to say that Garnett was completely unaware of the demands of the market. For example, he cut down D.H. Lawrence's *Sons and Lovers* partly because it was too long for the format of the book. But generally he was a champion of what he considered to be good writers.

SKB: Do you think editors like that still exist today?

HS: I think the role of editor has changed out of all recognition. Editors today don't do what Garnett did. They're just not there anymore, people like Garnett, people like Max Perkins in America. Publishing has changed so much. It's interesting to think what Garnett would have been if he were alive today. I think he would have been an agent rather than an editor.

SKB: In a letter to Garnett, Joseph Conrad wrote, 'you've made me.' What did he mean by that?

HS: I think he meant that Garnett made him as a writer. If you think about Conrad's situation when he met Garnett: he was a Polish merchant seaman in his late thirties, he had his maritime career, he'd finished one contract on a ship, hadn't got another, he'd written a first novel in his third language, and he was desperately, desperately short of confidence. He had no connections in the literary world and no confidence in his own writing. And he found Garnett who had the literary background, the literary connections and knew how to handle Conrad, knew how to coax him. Because Conrad was quite tricky. One wrong word and Garnett could have put him off writing altogether. But he was extraordinarily astute when it came to handling Conrad, he knew when to encourage, knew when to cajole him very gently, and propped him up in some terribly depressive times. Conrad writes to Garnett really quite graphic letters about how black his mood is, how he sits there for hour after hour trying to write and nothing happens. And during that time, Garnett really was an emotional crutch for Conrad. I think Conrad is the great example of how brilliant Garnett was at handling people, at knowing what to say and when to say it, and what tone to take with writers. Because his tone with Conrad is very different from what it was like with H.E. Bates, what it was like with both D.H. and T.E. Lawrence. So he had to be a terrifically good reader of people as well as a really good reader of manuscripts.

SKB: Garnett and Max Perkins were both considered to be 'authors' editors.' What is an author's editor? What qualities should they possess?

HS: If he were sitting here now, I think Garnett would say that an author's editor is somebody who looks after the author, whose first allegiance is to the author, not to the publisher. This got Garnett into some trouble in his career. His first loyalty was always to his writers never to his employer, and certainly Jonathan Cape got fed up with his maverick working tendencies at one point. But once he took someone on he was absolutely committed to them, and I think he saw that commitment not just to the writing but to the whole writing life, and that included the financial doldrums that many of his writers fell into while they were struggling to write books. The Irish writer Liam O'Flaherty springs to mind here. Garnett bought him a pair of false teeth, he bought him a bicycle, he advised him over his love life, he went and visited him in Ireland and nurtured him through the whole process. O'Flaherty was quite a difficult character in many ways. He'd been through the war. He suffered from what we now call post-traumatic stress disorder, his mood swings were extreme. And Garnett stood by him, held his hand, saw him through it all. So I think that's what Garnett would say an author's editor was: somebody whose absolute primary concern is the writer.

SKB: Garnett lived to 69 and it took you ten years to write about his life. What was it like to be working on one person's life for a decade?

HS: Well, I have to say that it shouldn't have taken ten years. A lot of things happened in my life during those ten years which meant that I had to take breaks from the book. But he was an extraordinarily interesting subject to write about and because he was dealing with so many different people it never got dull. There was plenty of variety in the personalities that he came into contact with, and they were so different which I think is a great testament to his skills as a mediator and mentor. So I never felt I'd had enough of him, that I just wanted to give him up or to get rid of him.

SKB: You were writing about someone who is dead and has been dead for a while. Elsewhere in this issue, Heather Martin writes about her biography of Lee Child, who is very much alive. Is it easier to write about someone who's dead?

HS: I think like most things there are advantages and disadvantages. Obviously, if someone's alive, you can get their side of things. You've got access to people who know them, which can of course cause its own complications. But it can also be very difficult writing about somebody who's living. I think the potential pitfalls probably outweigh the advantages. There's always the question of censorship. Does someone give you carte blanche to write about them and not worry about what's said and not want to see what you've written before it is published? And if they do and there's something in there that they want to suppress or they disagree with then obviously things can get quite tricky. So personally I prefer writing about the dead. And also if someone's dead, depending on how long they've been dead, you get a sense of perspective on their life and where they fit in with their times.

SKB: Garnett was an editor and a literary critic, but he also tried unsuccessfully to be a writer. How could he be such a successful editor and enabler of other people's careers yet be unable to find success as a writer?

HS: It was a source of great frustration to him that he couldn't write himself. But I think it's not an unfamiliar situation where you can spot something in other people and yet you know you can't do it yourself. If you're reading something it's there on the page in front of you and it has been created, and your job then is just to see where it works and where it doesn't. So maybe the problem with Garnett was actually getting to that point himself. D.H. Lawrence memorably said, 'Garnett ate his heart out trying to be a writer.' I think Garnett had ideas and he tried all sorts of genres. He wrote plays and he wrote a prose poem and he wrote a novel when he was very young, and none of them was much good. But it's a very interesting question about people who can immediately see what's wrong with somebody else's writing but they just can't successfully get to the stage of getting something down on the page themselves.

SKB: So would you agree that editing and writing are two completely separate skill sets?

HS: I think they probably are.

SKB: Would you ever consider becoming an editor or do you enjoy being a writer?

HS: I do quite a lot of editing in my professional role as a lecturer at the University of East Anglia. Every week on the non-fiction MA, students write pieces and I will read them and comment on them and edit them to a degree.

Writing is very hard. I find writing really hard. It takes me ages to write anything, absolutely ages. I really envy people who can write 1500 words a day just like that. Ford Madox Ford was one of those people. He had an amazing facility to write quickly. I haven't got that. Generally once I have written something it doesn't get edited much. Once I've finally wrenched it out of myself that tends to be it. The book that I submitted to Jonathan Cape was pretty much as I first wrote it.

SKB: *The Uncommon Reader* is 120,000 words long but neither your agent nor your editor did much editing on it? It was good to go?

HS: I was very fortunate in having Dan Franklin, who has since retired, as my editor. He was probably one of, if not *the*, preeminent editors in London, so I was quite anxious when my book finally landed on his desk what his reaction was going to be. I mean there were a few things, of course there were, but no major rewriting. So I was very lucky.

SKB: That's very surprising. I tend to write and write and then bin nearly all of it.

HS: I find that soul destroying. In one way you're very lucky and I wish I could do that but I can't. I think about things for absolutely ages, about the sentence structure and about words and about how to put things together. I've always been like that. But it's tortuous. When I was a student, I actually remember writing an essay for my MA and weeping at the kitchen table because I couldn't do it. I couldn't get the first words down on the paper. I did in the end. But there was just so much stuff going round in my head, writing something and then thinking, 'No, that's not right.'

SKB: So it has to be there in your head before you can put the first word down?

HS: The sentence has to emerge in my head to my satisfaction.

SKB: So on a day when you're working, what are the average number of words that you write?

HS: Gosh, I don't know, I've never really counted. Some days are easier than others. Some days I sit down and think this is a complete waste of time because I know I'm not going to produce anything at all. But if you think about writers like Arnold Bennett who decided, 'I am writing 1500 words in the morning and that's it,' I admire that enormously because I just couldn't do it. I couldn't write 1500 words day after day. I mean it's a terrific discipline to be able to do that I think, 1500 words every day. Like Edith Wharton, who used to write in the morning and then play society hostess in the afternoon.

SKB: Of course, they were writing fiction and you are writing non-fiction, and you must do a lot of research before you write a single sentence.

HS: And that's one of the pluses of writing fiction as opposed to non-fiction, possibly. But then look at someone like Flaubert who wrote painfully slowly. Scrupulous doesn't begin to describe how he was about his writing. I take your point about non-fiction having the research element and, yes, you're having to scrabble about looking for letters or looking for references. But one of the things I put quite a lot of emphasis on, rightly or wrongly, is thinking about how I can link things up so that one thing flows quite naturally into another. And that's quite difficult to do. So I don't think it would be fair to say that it's an entirely non-fiction thing because of the research. It's a thing about personality probably, and just how you're constituted.

SKB: A lot of *The Uncommon Reader* is based on letters to and from Garnett. Do you keep copies of your own letters and emails?

HS: No, I don't. We press the delete button on so many emails that it'll be interesting to see how biographers get on in future years. In one way, there's far more information out there now that any future biographer can find very easily. Think about the number of times you give details about yourself to any company or organisation. It's quite frightening. But there's a thing about physical letters. Is a biographer in 2080 going to enjoy the same kind of thrill reading a typed, electronic email that I've felt reading Garnett's letters where he's touched the paper, his pen has distributed ink on the page, where he's crossed things out? We just backspace and it's gone. So it may be easier but it may not be as rich.

SKB: As a lecturer in biography and creative non-fiction, would you agree that non-fiction and particularly life writing has surged in popularity over the last few years?

HS: I don't think there's any doubt about that. Non-fiction is incredibly in vogue at the moment. People may just be interested in things that have actually happened. Never forget that non-fiction and particularly biography is quite voyeuristic, and we're all incredibly nosy about other people's lives. One of the reasons we read non-fiction is to try and gain some kind of recognition of something in ourselves or in our own situation in the pages of the books that we're reading. That's one of the things I say to my students - although you're writing about something very particular to you, there has to be something within that writing that a reader can connect with and recognise. And really successful books do that.

SKB: There is a trend at the moment when writing biographies to include yourself within it as the researcher. You didn't do that in *The Uncommon Reader* but is it something you would consider in the future?

HS: Possibly. I don't think I'll do it in the next book because it wouldn't really fit. But I think also that, if you're going to do that, you need to do it with a purpose. I don't think people should just put themselves into a book for the sake of it. It has to have some real relevance to the book. It has to enhance the book in some way. But it comes down entirely to the form of non-fiction. I mean if you take *H is for Hawk* by Helen MacDonald, obviously she is central to the book. It's about her training the hawk but also about her grief on losing her father. People are also swayed by fashion and, as you say, at the moment it is very fashionable for biographers to include themselves in what they are writing. Doubtless, like all fashions, that will change.

SKB: There's also been some debate about crossing the gender line when doing biographies, that men shouldn't write about women's lives and vice versa. Do you have any comment on that?

HS: I never felt being a woman writing about a man disqualified me. I suppose to some extent it depends on your philosophy. Do you consider that men think and act in fundamentally different ways from women? And does the fact that you're a woman preclude you from being able to empathise with a male subject? I don't think it does but other people may disagree.

SKB: If you are looking for a biographical subject, what factors need to be in place to write a good book about them?

HS: There are so many things to take into consideration, one of which is have they been written about before and if they have, how recently? Certain figures have had countless biographies written about them: Shelley, Wordsworth, D.H. Lawrence. Conrad's had quite a few ...

SKB: Garnett's been written about before, in *Edward Garnett: A Life in Literature* by George Jefferson. Were you not wary of writing about him again?

HS: When I read that book I knew very little about him but I came away thinking, 'well I know quite a lot about him professionally from this book but I'm not terribly sure what he was like as a person.' I had various decisions to make about my book, one of which was how it was structured. George Jefferson's book is structured very much around the writers that he dealt with, so there was a chapter on Conrad and a chapter on Galsworthy, a chapter on Lawrence etc, and I can absolutely see why he did it. I decided against that for a couple of reasons, one of which was I think the whole reason that Garnett has been eclipsed in the past is because he has been overshadowed by the writers that he helped. He's kind of fallen into the background. And so I felt that giving those writers a chapter on their own actually does that all over again. It becomes a book of little vignettes of Conrad, of Lawrence, of Sean O'Faolain and whoever else.

I also thought that biography is about trying to give a taste of a life as it was lived, and that isn't how Garnett's life was. He didn't just have Conrad neatly boxed up and then move on to Galsworthy and then move on to D.H. Lawrence. He was dealing with Conrad simultaneously with Lawrence. Now I'm hard pressed to think of two more disparate characters than those two, and he's trying to juggle the demands of both of them at the same time. So I wanted to give a sense of just what it was like having to deal with all these people simultaneously. I've talked about Conrad and Lawrence and Galsworthy but there were so many other writers that he was dealing with and I wanted to give a sense of the chaos of trying to live your life with those personalities in it all at the same time.

SKB: You took a completely different approach.

HS: Yes. At the moment there's a big trend for people to write about figures in the voice of the person that they are writing about. In the new biography of Dylan Thomas that's exactly what the biographer tries to do, capture Thomas' voice and almost be inside his head. And I mean how do you write about somebody like Churchill who's been written about to death? If you want to write about Churchill how do you do it in a fresh way? Of course, if you've got new information and some treasure trove of archival sources that has never been seen before that's an enormous advantage. But for well-known figures most of those sources have been very well mined and there isn't any new material. So if you want to write about those people how do you do it? You've got to think of innovative ways to say something fresh about them or suggest new ways of looking at them.

SKB: Garnett was a very private man. He turned down honours, and at his funeral there was no service, no music and no speeches, and neither his wife nor his mistress attended. What do you think he would have made of your biography of him?

HS: Oh, he'd probably have growled and harrumphed and said it was a load of rubbish, I suspect. But there were moments in his career where he decried the amount of work he had to do, and the drudgery of it. He never made any money out of it, he was never well paid, he was never a wealthy man. And yet early twentieth century literature would look a lot different without him. And not just England, he did a lot for Irish writing, he introduced American writers over here, introduced Australian writers, he did a huge amount for literature in general. So I wonder if he might secretly have been a tiny bit gratified that his contribution has been highlighted.

The Uncommon Reader: A Life of Edward Garnett *is out now in hardback from Jonathan Cape.* **H**

Double page
spread,
full colour –
£350

Single page,
full colour –
£200

Half page,
full colour –
£120

Single page,
b&w – £150

Half page,
b&w – £70

To take advantage of the above rates and advertise
with Hinterland, or to discuss sponsorship
or other collaborations, please contact
Andrew Kenrick: hinterlandnonfiction@gmail.com